GLIMPSES

GLIMPSES

PAT FOWLE

Matador
9 Priory Business Park,
Wistow Road, Kibworth Beauchamp,
Leicestershire. LE8 0RX
Tel: 0116 279 2299
Email: books@troubador.co.uk
Web: www.troubador.co.uk/matador
Twitter: @matadorbooks

ISBN 978 1 8031 3038 5

British Library Cataloguing in Publication Data.
A catalogue record for this book is available from the British Library.

Printed and bound by CPI Group (UK) Ltd, Croydon, CR0 4YY
Typeset in 11pt Minion Pro by Troubador Publishing Ltd, Leicester, UK

Matador is an imprint of Troubador Publishing Ltd

This book is for my nine grandchildren.

GLIMPSES

This is a glimpse into what I consider to be noteworthy memories. Most of one's life is not always memorable. I spent a fair amount of my past just chasing the wind, however, I can recall certain events, some of which I will relate to you. I'll stick to glimpses, since I do not intend for these recollections of my life to read like a diary.

I will start at the very beginning and recount briefly, my earliest memory. I was sitting outside my house in a pram, aggressively objecting to anyone who passed too near. In contrast, I remember looking down at our cat lying close to the pram and feeling affection towards it. Not an exciting first account, but there it is, first memory! I have fleeting memories of my infant school in Cambridge, which I recall as being on the whole enjoyable. The second strong memory is of my maternal great-grandmother, known to the family as 'Little Granny'. She was very old. My grandmother told me she was one hundred years old. Apparently, she had never been ill and had never had to see a doctor. One fact remained clear to me – she loved humbugs. Round-shaped sweets with stripes running through like rock! Popular in those days.

One very cold and frosty day, Little Granny decided to make a trip to the nearby corner shop. She had run out of humbugs and the corner shop she knew supplied them.

The pavements on that day were dangerously icy but unperturbed. Little Granny set off for the short distance to get her one indulgence: humbugs. With the icy conditions making walking on foot treacherous, she soon slipped and fell, breaking her arm in the process. An ambulance was called and the last we ever saw of Little Granny was (and this is what I clearly remember) of her smiling and waving cheerfully with the good arm. It was seeing her seated alone inside the dark, old-fashioned ambulance, smiling so bravely as the doors closed and she was driven away, that affected me deeply. I'm trying to remember what I felt at the time; affection, yes; compassion, I don't know. I didn't think then that she shouldn't have gone unaccompanied to the hospital – I was four years old! I do now. Little Granny died a few days later of pneumonia. No antibiotics then. I recall now that my grandmother always found it difficult and sad to say goodbye. I remember her chin used to wobble without fail when saying goodbye to anyone and everyone.

I don't remember that I spent a great deal of time at Addenbrooke's Hospital, Cambridge, when I was a baby. Glandular problems, possibly due to unpasteurised milk. I also had a long stay once again at four or possibly just five. I was put into the children's ward with scarlet fever and, due to it being the contagious ward, it followed on with measles and a few other unwelcome diseases. I do remember some of my time there as being happy, thanks to the wonderful nurses and doctors, especially on Christmas day when Father Christmas arrived on the ward and gave everyone a present. Because it was a contagious ward, no one was allowed to have toys to take home and my teddy bear was removed and, I was told, destroyed. One of my less happy memories.

In 1940 I went to London with my mother and her lover, to live. I was just four when the second world war broke out, experiencing what all children at that time did: rationing, air raids, nearby shelters to run to. I recall a bombing from time to time and yet my childhood was for most of the time, happy! I should mention now that due to my father's kind heart, my whole life was changed forever. It was during a short leave from the army that my father met, on a train from London to Cambridge, a lonely young man. He invited him to stay at our home for the weekend. "Poor fellow," my father had said to my mother. "Make him feel at home." Those were the parting words from my foolish father, as he left to return to camp. Well! My mother did. She was very young, twenty-three and very attractive, and the tall, dark, handsome man was charming. They started an affair and soon fled to London, taking me with them. I was then five and it was 1940. Some months after, my father was given compassionate leave to find me, which he did effortlessly. Thanks to my grandmother, who had the address, he swiftly deposited me at my maternal grandmother's small house and there, thank God, I remained for the rest of my school days. My father was an unassuming sort of man, ill-equipped for this world, but I hero-worshipped him.

The next vivid memory which has stayed with me was on my seventh birthday. I remember standing close to a vegetable patch in my aunt's garden. I remember smiling with great concentration at the box camera my aunt was holding – *click*, as the mechanism went into action. I clicked into a sudden awareness at the very same moment. *I am seven and I am in this world.* The realisation of this thought flooded over me for the first time in my life. There was something else I felt and almost knew in that instant. I hovered on the threshold of a stillness, waiting. I held my breath in an effort not to think or breathe. The strange feeling passed almost in the same second. I smiled now at my aunt and not the camera. I asked if I could keep the photograph to put in my album. I didn't in fact have an album at the time, but my aunt nodded anyway. Aunt Gladys was my mother's sister and was an extremely organised person with a good, solid character. She made most of my clothes as well as for her two daughters. The youngest of whom I had, and still have, a great affection for. What I most admired about my aunt was her ability to knit and read at the same time. As for my grandmother, she was a busy, industrious woman who struggled cheerfully to make ends meet. I know that she was fond of me. It was just that she didn't have the enthusiasm, or perhaps the energy, to show it. One didn't show much outward sign of affection in those days!

She was small and moved quickly like a nervous bird. Her nose was slightly hooked. She had small, dark eyes that were set quite deeply in her tiny, wrinkled face, brown from hours in the sun attending to vegetables, fruit, chickens and rabbits and one very privileged duck. Almost every inch of the garden was used for practical purposes, with one exception. A small patch kept clear for Lily of the valley, which reappeared every year roundabout May. It seemed to be the only softness she allowed herself. Granny enjoyed the exquisite perfume for a short while. Just once a year.

At the age of eleven, almost twelve, I suddenly decided I wanted to go to a catholic school. I'm not sure how or why this came about, only that I was very determined. My granny just ignored me, but my father couldn't. I was too persistent. I persuaded him to make a telephone call which resulted in an interview. We were not practising Catholics, however, to my delight and gratitude, I was accepted. A longer walk to school was involved, but I didn't mind – I was happy!

The years passed as time and my grandmother nurtured me through to the blossoming of adolescence. My album, which I finally acquired, was more than half full now. It was always kept in an old chest of drawers in my bedroom. From time to time, it would be taken out and an important event, such as a day by the sea or a school outing, would be carefully pasted onto the pages. I remember very clearly an experience which brings me to another strong memory.

It was the long holiday. I had almost reached the age of fifteen. I was happy and carefree, enjoying the long, warm summer. Most afternoons were spent at an outdoor swimming pool. Not so much for the healthy exercise but for the after-event. The pool was set in a large park with weeping willows and well-tended beds of varying shrubs and flowers. I would wander through the park with my friends after our swim, with damp rolled towels tucked under our arms, to select a nice shady tree. Cheeks glowing from the warm sun and hair still damp from swimming, we would sit and talk and laugh a great deal. We were waiting for the boys to swagger over to where we sat. This was the most exciting time. The afternoon sun, gentle now, shone on the polished bicycles of the casual boys as they stood a short distance from us, joking and teasing, asking impertinent questions with an air of disinterest and a strong hint of sarcasm. We answered in the same offhand, unserious manner. I hated leaving before the others, but I had to be home at a certain time. My route home was always the same: across the park to a small path beside a narrow stream. It led to the main road where I would cross to the other side and enter, having first opened an old rusty gate onto a wide stretch of common land. I would then cut across the common to another busy road and it was just five minutes' walk to my house. I always walked alone and rather enjoyed it. I would often think about what smart replies I might have given to the handsome boy who teased me so much. One evening, as I made my way home – rather in haste as the sun was beginning to set, leaving me with a slight feeling of panic and desertion – I remember pulling open the rusty old gate, which felt uncomfortable to touch. The rust and broken pieces of metal dug into my hand, making me wipe it on my dress. I began to walk at a brisk pace, trying to make up for lost time. It was at that moment I experienced the same feeling I had half a lifetime ago. When I was seven, standing by the vegetable patch, a strange stillness, a waiting, only this time, though, there was more than that. An awareness of something wonderful. I was suddenly filled with indescribable joy. This feeling began to fade as I approached the main road. Then I was as I had been before entering through the gate, just concerned about arriving home on time. The following evening, I slipped through the gate and on to the common. As I walked a short distance, the now familiar awareness flooded over me. It made me feel buoyant and almost bursting with happiness. A feeling of love poured from my heart with great force and yet again, as I reached the busy traffic laden road, the other-worldly feeling had passed. It left me with knowing that I was not ready. I didn't question this or talk about my experience to anyone. It never happened crossing the common again. So much time had passed and still that memory remains crystal clear.

I lived for most of my seventeenth year in Casablanca, Morocco, with an English family as a 'Mother's help'. I always longed to travel to see the world and working for a family was, for me, the only way to do it. Maybe I was too young because I certainly became homesick. I wanted so much to return home to my grandmother, cat, dog, rabbits, chickens, plum tree. I don't know what homesickness really is. I do know that after only about three days it was well and truly quelled, and I set about planning my next adventure. However, not long after my return from Casablanca, I met my soulmate. It was in October of 1953. This is a bit cheesy but a completely true account of how I met my husband, Richard.

It was about the beginning of the autumn term when I decided to go with several of my girlfriends to the university jazz club. I loved jazz and enjoyed the atmosphere and the live music. It was during the interval when a record player was substituted for the next twenty minutes or so. It was playing 'Blue Moon'. I was standing on a chair at the time, which allowed me to look around the crowded room from an advantaged position. I suppose I was influenced by the words of the song, *you heard me saying a prayer for* because I did, in fact, say a prayer for someone to care for and to care for me. My prayer, which was rather impatient, was answered instantly. A student attempting to grow his first moustache arrived at my side and asked me for a dance. His name was Richard. Four years later, we were married.

CUPID'S DART

I don't remember the exact date, somewhere around the early spring of 1954. My boyfriend Richard used to park around the corner from where I lived. He had a sportly green Wolseley Hornet Special. I have to admit that I was very impressed by that car. Most of the students got around satisfactorily on bicycles. My grandmother could never come to terms with me having anything to do with the opposite sex. That's why Richard always parked out of sight. He would wait for me to turn up at our arranged time. I was always a little late and he was always patient and on time. On this particular occasion, I was walking my grandmother's dog 'Trixie', a black cocker spaniel. We were returning from a walk on Midsummer Common. I reached the car and told Richard that I would deposit Trixie, then return. I walked briskly towards the corner, which was a short distance, some fifty yards. It was at that moment I felt a love so strong that it seemed to lift me off the ground as I walked. At the same time, it felt as though a dart or something sharp had pierced my back, lifting me further away from the ground. I disappeared from Richard's view around the corner and the sensation ceased at the same moment. It all happened in a few seconds. Minutes later, I was back at the car and ready to enjoy our date. I didn't mention this strange experience to Richard or anyone. However, years after, I don't remember how many, we were married with three children. We were just sitting together reminiscing about past times when my husband, out of the blue, said, "I remember very vividly on one occasion, when I was waiting for you in my car. You had been taking Trixie for a walk on the common and, as you walked away from me, I had such an overwhelming feeling of love for you. I seemed to be floating behind you until you went around the corner and out of sight. I then told him of my experience and we both realised that we had shared something very special. We seemed to share quite a few experiences, including several dreams. But dreams are dreams!

In the late July of 1954, I was eighteen, almost nineteen, years of age and life, I thought, was pretty good. For the past few months, I had been working as an apprentice in a jewellery shop in the centre of Cambridge. To be an apprentice meant being paid less wage. A clever ruse on the part of the employer.

My boyfriend Richard had been an undergraduate at Trinity College. He had just graduated and left to take his place in the world of exploration geophysics. A fascinating life lay ahead of Richard and, in due course, I was to share that future with him.

My free half day from the jewellery shop was Thursday afternoons. I looked forward to this time of being alone for a short while. I still lived with my grandmother, whose once-a-week social club fortunately coincided with my half day off. I would always sit on the same hard wooden chair in the small sitting room. On this particular Thursday, it was the usual time of about 2pm. I remember the inside of the house was cool and dark, in fact, quite gloomy in contrast to the bright sunlight in the garden. I used this time to contemplate, and my train of thought was always the same. I could believe that God 'is', and always will be, but couldn't get my head around God always 'was'. I could not fathom God always being and yet believed without any doubt that he 'is'! It didn't make a great deal of sense to me. That's why I would pursue this same thought over and over. I tried to imagine nothing existing except one entity, perhaps in some kind of shape or form. Perhaps just spirit or space. No one except Jesus has ever seen God, and we as mortals need an image to work on. My limited mind simply would not or could not comply. However, I believed by my faith that God exists. Again and again, I reached the barrier put up by my logical mind aided and abetted by reasoning. Each time I would start over from the beginning, still trying to rationalise the thought of God always being. It had always been an impossible task for the mind. However, on that special afternoon when I once more reached the barrier, I somehow knew how to abandon my logic and reasoning and was then allowed to penetrate and pass the threshold of my senses.

I will endeavour to write a true account as best as I can, given that my memory at the time of the experience allowed only certain fragments to remain. My soul or spirit (or both) seemed to be released from my body, taking flight from somewhere between my temples. Throughout the whole experience, I'm sure I remained physically unmoving on the wooden chair. My spirit was taken up to a high place and from there, I was shown. Because clearly, I was, but by whom or what I don't know. In front of me I saw what looked like a high wall embedded with stones of various colours. I travelled downwards until I reached the ground. From there, I was allowed to look through a large gate or door. But was not allowed to enter. I don't know what I saw inside that gate or door, but I do remember very clearly thinking that it was all perfect and for some reason, I received the knowledge that all was well, that all would be well.

The second part is really difficult to explain. It was too sacred for words and yet it remains the most endearing experience of my life. Somehow, I was a short distance away but clearly observing my soul or spirit standing in light outside somewhere that might have been a patio. My spirit then merged with my soul or vice versa and I became immersed in the light. I then became one with the light and began to soar upwards towards the source. I felt such a deep yearning for the love I felt. Never before or since have I known such a longing. It was too ineffable to put into words. A clear voice inside me said, "You can go on and know, but life will never be the same." I don't know why I felt afraid, but I did. I thought possibly that I might die in the process. I replied in the same way, silently, that I was not ready and wanted to live my life in this world, even if it was not always happy. Before I could even complete the thought, I was back in my little room. I know I haven't explained all this adequately, but there are no words to describe such love. I've never stopped feeling guilty that I didn't have the courage or sufficient love to go on. This happened when I was eighteen years of age. I am now eighty-five! I left my grandmother's house that afternoon aware that even though the sun was shining, how grey everything appeared in contrast to what had just happened. I was still hugging the amazing gift of love I had received. I was not special in any way. I had certainly done nothing to deserve this love. I did have a strong faith but that is also a gift! It was my fourth other-worldly experience and by far the most wonderful.

I didn't tell anyone what had happened that Thursday afternoon, with the exception of my boyfriend Richard. I visited him the following weekend at his home in Surrey and shared my experience. The extraordinary thing was that he too had something similar happen to him at about the same time on the same day. He described it as being absorbed by the universe. He, unlike me, was reluctant to return to this world. But he didn't seem to have the choice. I don't know why I received this love, or why I didn't pursue the light when invited. I know for sure that I didn't deserve such a gift. About eighteen months before this amazing experience, I was walking past the Catholic church in Cambridge when I suddenly sensed a holy presence for just a few seconds. My silent reply was: *give me another year*. I was given that time and still declined.

Catholic doctor, Dr Patrick Pullincio, says that he is convinced that there are two spirits in the body. The bodily spirit and the soul, the divine spirit. I absolutely agree!

Richard had graduated and left university. He started work almost immediately as a geophysicist based, for a short time, in London, before embarking on more exciting, and sometimes outlandish, places. I moved to London as a few of my friends had decided to do the same thing. I enjoyed my time there even though I would often have to forgo a meal or two for a new dress or shoes! After a while, I began to feel restless. Richard had gone off to the Near East on a two-year contract, so I decided to visit Casablanca again, this time with my room-mate and best friend Helen. I was last there in 1952/1953.

It was now 1956. Life had changed a great deal in Morocco. Having got its independence, almost all the French had left. Getting a labour permit was not easy, in fact it was impossible if it were not for the American embassy, who were extremely helpful. Without them, we would not have found temporary work. It enabled us to save just enough to make the journey home. After a few weeks of baby caring and attempting office work, I may have done more damage than good with my clerical input. Having saved barely enough to return to England, we set off to Tangiers by coach. From there, a boat to Gibraltar, and finally a ferry to Spain. From there, the walking began. Transport seemed to be in short supply in Southern Spain. In retrospect, our adventures through Spain, but mostly in France, were often risky and just a few of the lifts we were given had without doubt a menacing atmosphere. However, we survived unscathed. I truly felt we had been protected in some way and was thankful. I was sort of sad when we reached England, unlike my friend who was openly relieved and waved goodbye to me very happily when we parted at the railway station. Helen was glad to be going home. I continued to work and live in London until I got married in March 1958. I have to say that the big city was never really for me. I seemed to suffer more than others from pollution. My eyes never stopped stinging, my nose permanently blocked. Our first posting together, which was living in the heat of Baghdad, Iraq, suited me far more than the UK climate.

I was almost four months pregnant when we arrived in Baghdad, about one week before their not entirely bloodless revolution. The coup d'état happened on the 14th of July

1958, during the early hours of the morning, whilst we were sound asleep. It resulted successfully in the overthrow of the British-installed Hashemite monarchy. It was brought to power by Iraq military officers, led by Abd al-Karim Qasim. Prince Faisal and his uncle attempted to escape by disguising themselves as women, complete with yashmaks. They didn't make it and ended up with their heads displayed on street lamps! I found the curfews prohibiting movements very trying. It went on for a long time. My husband continued with his work, going away for about three weeks at a time. He would come home for no more than five days, then off again. Meanwhile, I had at least twenty American marines who were attached to the American embassy. They lived in a large house just across the road from us. It was without doubt comforting to know they were a short distance away, complete with guns and more, but at the same time I sometimes felt a little disturbed by their unwanted attentions.

One memory of Baghdad, which still makes me sad, is of two little carefree puppy dogs. They lived three houses away. They were of mixed breed and were as cute as only puppies can be. About two weeks after the revolution, the American couple who were the owners of the puppies were ordered at short notice to return to the USA. They left the pups in the not-so-capable hands of their cook, who had been paid in advance to look after them. In no time, the money ran out and the helpless pups were hurled out into the street, left to fend for themselves. At first, they seemed carefree and playful. Someone without doubt was feeding them. It was not the cook. It turned out to be the kind doctor who lived further along the street. Sleeping rough, they were prone to all sorts of diseases and accidents. The doctor had told me firmly not to get involved with them. The more dominant of the two was limping badly and was now no longer the top dog. Both were now miserably thin. The doctor had the injured dog put down, which left the rather timid one to struggle alone. That's when I started to feed him in my small front garden. He looked too bedraggled and mangey to invite inside our bungalow. I think someone may have poisoned him. It might have actually been the doctor being kind, because he had shown signs of having rabies. He finally died in my front garden, next to his water bowl. Not a good memory. They were two innocent victims of the revolution.

I found the Iraqi people to be intelligent and most of the time very friendly. Some were wary of getting too close. The propaganda on the radio had a lot to do with their attitude. One day, I would be labelled a British imperialist. The next day, better if I said I was Russian. Not the fault of the Iraqi people! Most of the power-thirsty everywhere eventually get their comeuppance.

On the advice of Richard's company, we went to Kirkuk, North Iraq, to have our first baby. But whilst waiting day by day for the impending birth, a huge problem arose when Richard suddenly contracted hepatitis A and was very ill. I had to escort him into the hospital from the guest house where we were staying. It was a short distance and we managed to walk there. I was unceremoniously dismissed from my husband's room on the grounds that I might be infected by him. I tried to explain that we shared the same room and bed, but to no avail. Rules are rules I was told firmly. So, I returned to my lonely room to await my son's arrival. It happened about forty-eight hours later. We were deprived of sharing the joy of our son's birth together. Richard was introduced to him on the second day. He peered in silent wonderment at our baby then simply said, "He looks like your father!"

The weather was pleasantly cooler, although the political situation was still a little heated. Curfew regulations were still in operation. In-between curfew hours, we managed to get out and about. When Richard was home, we occasionally went to Babylon for an ant-infected picnic. Some parts of the Procession Street still existed then, although now in unrecognisable ruins. Ancient Babylon is, or was, situated on the banks of the Euphrates, about sixty miles South of Baghdad. The site was restored by Saddam Hussain, who built a palace there. In April 2003, US marines under John Coleman stormed up to Euphrates valley and turned Saddam's palace into a camp for some two thousand American troops. Saddam had done some very impressive restoration, especially the Processional Way. A report by the British museum's John Curtis was depressing. Large areas had been covered in gravel, destructive procedures done to provide helipads, car parks, etc. US military vehicles had destroyed 2,600 brick pavements. Trenches dug into ancient deposits. Bricks with Nebuchadnezzar's name filled sandbags. But the worst part was the damage to areas which had never been excavated, secrets of Babylon. The hanging gardens may never be found! Troops should not have been allowed to take home some of the irreplaceable objects as souvenirs. By 2003, Babylonian cuneiform tablets (the oldest examples of writing) were being sold on ebay.

So will Babylon the great city be thrown down with violence, and will be found no more.

REVELATION 18:21

When we were there over sixty years ago, the Lion of Babylon was, despite his 2,600 years, still in very good fettle!

Our son was now four months old, and we were heading home. It felt good! Our chains had been removed and we were returning to freedom. I know I'm using a strong metaphor that makes it sound dramatic, but that's how it felt! Our son put on a good display of volume! He yelled non-stop from the moment we stepped on the plane, until the excellent Dutch airline staff rigged up a swinging hammock just above our seats. It was magic! He stopped crying, smiled at us as he swung gently to and fro, then fell fast asleep for the rest of the flight.

I pass grey skies and perfumed mayflowers of England to bring you to my next adventure, which was Pakistan. On reflection, I think it was my favourite posting. Why? Well, I know now that it doesn't always matter where you are. It's a state of mind, and mine of that time was obviously at its happiest. We spent a few weeks in Karachi, still too hot for comfort. My husband went up north ahead of me. I followed on about three weeks later. The Punjab, when I arrived, was cooler. The fans had been turned off. We were housed in a nice little stone bungalow with a fireplace for the evening winter fires. The kitchen, for some reason, was separated by about twenty yards or so from the bungalow. Richard was away during the week working near the salt range hills. There were very few people left at the camp. However, I never suffered from loneliness. There was always something to do, and I had a toddler which really kept me occupied. We bought a large rocking horse made locally from a family who were returning to the UK. Our son, Michael, loved it. It provided hours of enjoyment.

Thank goodness no sign of a threatening revolution, all was calm! Just lovely wood fire scents burning in otherwise unpolluted air. The mali (gardener) checks his personal patch of garden daily, kept clear for growing chillies. The pace of life was not hurried. Maybe that's what I liked so much. After a few hours' drive, one could see the foothills of the Himalayas. It was simply beautiful! Abounding with wild fragrant flowers. I even took up horse riding in a not-too-serious way. Truth is, I was terrified of the horses given to me to exercise, they seemed huge! And no amount of congealed brown sugar offered to them for enticement could improve my confidence. The odd cobra alarmed me on rare occasions. They would approach the warmth of the kitchen, especially in the cooler months. I only saw two and they slithered away at the vibration of footsteps approaching, which I suppose was lucky for me! I then understood the possible reason for separate kitchens. We were truly sad to say goodbye to the good people in North Pakistan, and this we did whilst being presented with flowered garlands placed with dignified courtesy over our heads. We returned to Karachi and then on to Malaya to spend Christmas with my sister-in-law and her husband. All I seem to remember about that very short visit was the rather impressive golf course housing more than its fair share of poisonous snakes. There were quite a few monkeys, but I was more preoccupied with not stepping on a snake.

Malayan food I found delicious. They also imported beef and sponge cakes and other long-forgotten luxuries. Our next and third posting was Papua, New Guinea, Port Moresby to be precise. It was very different to anything I'd ever seen before. Heavily pregnant women clothed only in a skirt, naked from the waist up and happily eating ice cream cones which they had just bought from the one and only ice-cream parlour. We all queued together for this treat! A young man, fresh from the mission hostel, was sent to help us. At first, I found him disturbing in that he had a large bone through his nose. I found it difficult to take my eyes off this spectacle when trying to communicate, and although he couldn't read, he held a bible in his hands most of the time, even when attempting to carry out a chore. I always thought that his strong heritage of witchcraft was still way ahead of his Christian belief, but perhaps time would tell!

Richard worked most of the time from home, which was a treat for me. Sometimes he would go out to sea for offshore seismic work. On those occasions, which lasted for a few days at a time, I would sleep with a heavy object under my pillow! I was glad to leave Port Moresby after six months. I was expecting our second child, Shanny, and was anxious to move on. Our young man with the bible had taken to leaving dead snakes on the doorstep. I don't know if this was protection or a threat. I didn't ask!

We bought a little shiny red car for our son, Michael, who was just two years old. He spent endless hours pedalling up and down our house which was built on sticks. It did in fact have vast space for him to play. He was very adept at mimicking the local taxi drivers and used to invite us into his little red car by opening the side door. I looked forward to our fourth posting!

After a few weeks' leave in England, we were off again to our next posting. The year was 1961 and we were going to Rangoon (now Yangon) in Burma, now called Myanmar. I liked the Burmese very much. They were cheerful, polite, and in those days, all was peaceful. My husband, as always, learned the language quite quickly. I gave up lessons after three weeks when I was approaching lesson three: 'Can you pluck this plum from the tree with a forked stick?'. I decided to give up there and then, no perseverance!

The most amazing wonder was, to me, the sight of the Shwedagon Pagoda in Rangoon (Yangon.) Gilded with gold leaf, it was built 2,500 years ago. Almost as old as the The Lion of Babylon! It had been renovated several times in the past and was the most famed Buddhist pagoda in Burma. The British army had not long left, and they did so peacefully. We always seemed to arrive wherever political changes were taking place. Our daughter Shanny was delivered at the Prone Road nursing home in Rangoon on the 21st of September 1961. Despite the efforts of my doctor, she was born at 12.30am, half an hour after my birthday. From the very beginning, she had a cheerful disposition and still has that happy personality today. I really believe that you can tell from the very beginning what their personalities are going to be like. Our son Michael seemed very happy in Rangoon and learned to speak Burmese from the age of three, thanks to our nanny who was a Karen and spoke very good English. She had worked with British army families for many years. Burma was a good posting. Lots going on with an active social life. My husband worked for a good, solid, old-fashioned company, which on occasions reminded me of how I imagined old colonial days and how it might have been in the past. March 1962 was the end of democratic rule in Burma as the win overthrew the international control commission, all peacefully. By the time we left Burma in 1963, I was expecting our third child Wendy. We returned to the UK and set about finding a house as soon as possible. I was seven and a half months pregnant. We soon found a suitable house. It was brand new, and it was quite near Richard's parents. Although sparsely furnished, it felt good to have our own house for the first time. Wendy was born leisurely in our bed in Woking. Not as exotic as her brother's and sister's births. She, however, flourished happily in her leafy Surrey environment.

There, we remained in Woking for a few years, before setting off once again on our adventures, this time to Ecuador, South America. Our fifth posting, we set off from Southampton to New York on the old *Queen Elizabeth II*, a great experience for the family. I confess happily to being a landlubber and have always preferred terra firma!

We arrived in New York to what must have been a heatwave, or perhaps it was just that the month was August. It was unbearably hot! Our hotel fortunately had good air conditioning, as did the shops, stores and restaurants. We visited the Empire State Building. Our two days in New York were stimulating, despite the extreme heat. We flew to Miami and stayed long enough to be introduced to 'Flipper', a famous dolphin. It was a great favourite with my children who had become acquainted with his regular appearances on British television. Flipper did not disappoint. He performed to perfection in anticipation of the juicy fish that was his reward.

Our first stay in Ecuador was by the sea about sixty miles from Guayaquil. We stayed for only five months then returned to England. A month later, we went back to Ecuador, this time to Quito, which was at an altitude of 9,350 feet. The second highest city in the world. We were there for just over two years. It was a fascinating colonial city, surrounded by snow-capped mountains, including the most impressive, 'Cotopaxi'. It was a perfect setting situated on the equator which, due to the altitude, was never too hot. It did rain, though, without fail, every afternoon. I don't know why, but I didn't enjoy that posting so much. Perhaps it was at a different time of my life. Maybe it was the altitude. Or perhaps it was because we thought it was necessary to leave our young son Michael behind in England at boarding school. We were too far away from him for comfort. Whatever the reason, I did not feel happy! We managed to learn a little Spanish. My husband outshining us all with his gift for languages, or maybe he just persevered more. The girls went first to an American school and then private tuition with three other children. Fortunately, they all seemed happy with this arrangement. I remember an enjoyable event which was on the 4th of July. It was a celebration fete, and my husband and I won the egg-throwing competition. I still have the trophy.

THE WEDDING

I will relate the story of a wedding we attended. I can't remember the date but remember it all very well. I have quite a few memories of my two years in Quito, Ecuador. One event I clearly recall was a wedding that I was invited to with my husband. He was to be the *padrino* and I, the *madrina* (best man and, I suppose, best woman).

The wedding was to take place in a small village, home of the bride's parents which was in the Oriente, the upper Amazon. We set off from our home in Quito in good spirits with our two young daughters. Our son was ensconced at school in England.

The drive down the Andes was fascinating as well as hair-raising since the route had a notorious weakness for landslides. However, we only encountered one recent landslide and arrived safely, although hot and dusty, at the one and only small hotel.

The bride and groom-to-be were also staying at the same hotel and had arranged a small party that evening. It was the day before the wedding. His name was Jerry, a cheerful, charming character, but well past the first flush of youth!

His bride-to-be, on the other hand, was very young and extremely pretty. She spoke only Spanish and he, a Canadian, understood very little of that flowery language. I can't remember how they met, but one thing was sure: that they communicated satisfactorily with the universal language of love. Late that evening, after having refreshed ourselves and eaten, we joined the party in the bar. Jerry was there with his intended, Maria, and most of her family, which numbered more than a few.

But imagine our surprise as we entered into what we thought would be a happy gathering, to find long, unhappy faces, and worse, the bride-to-be and her sister in floods of tears. When we asked what the matter was, they all proceeded to explain at once. Now, I have to admit that my Spanish was very limited, however my husband fortunately had a stronger grasp of the language, and so between us, we understood that the wedding could not take place the following day because our friend Jerry had been divorced. Therefore, the local Catholic priest refused to marry them. After a brief discussion, we all reviewed the sad situation over a drink, and then suddenly, out of the blue, I had a brainwave.

"Were you married in a church or a registry office?" I asked excitedly.

"Registry office," Jerry replied heavily.

"That's it then," I yelled triumphantly. "In the eyes of the church, you were never actually married at all. In which case, you could never have been divorced."

Everyone cheered up. It seemed there was hope again. First thing in the morning, Jerry and Maria would go to the priest and explain the situation.

The following morning, my husband took the girls out

for a drive around to see the banana and tea plantations. My main concern was to find the hairdresser. There was only one, run by a couple of retired ladies, from a profession, I was told, 'less said, sooner mended'.

The establishment was basic to say the least. One hairdryer and a seriously cracked washbasin greeted me. I strongly doubted that the ladies knew a great deal about the care or appearance of hair. However, it was a matter of take it or leave it, and so I sat at their mercy. Less than five minutes after being placed under the hairdryer, the electricity failed, and although both ladies shook their heads in exasperation, they said this was not unusual. Apparently, the electricity was always failing. I was deciding what to do next when a rather breathless Jerry and Maria arrived.

"You must come with us immediately, please!" Jerry pleaded when he had recovered his breath. "The priest wants to talk to you. It's so important that you try to convince him!"

I didn't even have time to take out my rollers, but at least I had a scarf to cover my embarrassment, and so, trying to look as dignified as possible in the circumstances, I was taken to a house in the village and shown into a small room darkened by partially drawn curtains. The priest half rose to greet us from his comfortable armchair. I imagined his enormous stomach hindered any hope of agility. To my dismay, he spoke only Spanish, or perhaps it was to my advantage because after only about ten minutes trying to explain that Jerry had never actually been married in the eyes of the Catholic church, the priest finally smiled. Admittedly, it was only a thin smile, but it was encouraging. He then raised his hand, either in resignation or to stop my flow of imperfect Spanish, and agreed to marry the couple that same evening.

Mission accomplished, I returned to the hairdresser's shack. The electricity was working again and soon after, I was set free with a hairstyle, of sorts, into the narrow street. As I started back to the hotel, it began to rain. My scarf did little to protect me from the deluge that descended. By the time I'd reached the hotel, the rain had stopped. Under the soaked scarf, my hair was a dripping disaster.

I found my husband and children happily wandering around the damp lush garden, enjoying the splendid display of orchids. They also discovered a cage which housed two lively monkeys. We stood and watched them for some time. Excellent therapy for the nerves. I even forgot to worry about my hair.

The wedding was to be at 9pm. A strange hour, we thought, but we were told it was quite normal for this part of the world. We arrived well on time at the arranged place, which was a small convent. Our daughters were placed in seats at the front and nuns bustled to and fro, arranging flowers and smiling placidly. One came towards me and very gently placed me next to the nervous and slightly confused bridegroom. It was embarrassingly obvious that she had mistaken me for the bride. The arrival of the real McCoy sorted out that little mistake and finally, the bride and groom stood resolutely side by side. My husband and I stood stiffly to attention, me next to the bride and he, next to the groom. I soon felt myself being firmly pushed to one side to allow the bride's father to claim his rightful place next to his daughter.

At last, the ceremony was ready to begin. The bride looked absolutely beautiful in a flowing white gown, which was a mixture of lace and cotton. The veil was a handmade work of art. Incredibly delicate and typically South American in design. The bridesmaids stood behind us in crisp blue dresses. Hair immaculately arranged, which is more than I could say for the *madrina*. I wondered how it was possible to look like something out of *Vogue* in this little village where most of the wooden houses were crudely made and stood on sticks at irregular angles.

The priest was ready. He seemed peacefully detached from the whole scene as he gazed beyond us all. His face shone with moisture as perspiration poured freely down to his collar. More in haste than habit I felt. He began to mumble in Spanish the words of the most holy sacrament of marriage. As he did so, a small mangy-looking dog appeared, as if from nowhere, and began sniffing around energetically, quite obviously looking for something specific. Well, he found it when he reached the priest's cassocks.

The miserable dog just lifted his leg and relieved himself. The priest swiftly kicked the unfortunate animal, without so much as a glance down, and continued the service. I felt hysterical laughter rising uncontrollably inside me and fought to overcome it. Thank goodness I succeeded.

After the ceremony, we collected the girls, then made our way to the reception being held at a hall in the village which was the property of the local police. We arrived to find guests already seated, males one side of the room and females on the other. Our timing was good. Champagne was being handed around and we grabbed a glass each as the tray passed and had gulped at least half of it down before the small band started up. Now, I love South American music, but the volume of that tiny band was unbelievable. Everyone got up to dance and Jerry left his radiant bride's side to join us for a moment.

"I want to thank you both for all your help and support," he said, his face glowing with happiness. He raised his glass before us in a toast and we muttered self-consciously, saying something like 'what are friends for?'.

"Just as well I didn't mention my other marriage," Jerry grinned cheerfully.

"What other marriage?" I asked weakly, when I'd finished mopping up my spilt drink.

"My first marriage – a complete disaster. Now that one was in a church." Jerry looked adoringly across the room at his lovely young bride. "Must go." He beamed and left us with the deafening music and a distinct feeling of guilt.

THE GROUP

One of my great friends in Quito was an Austrian woman named Hede. She was married to an American, but sadly they divorced soon after leaving Ecuador. Hede was most definitely imperious. She certainly didn't lack confidence. I found her very kind and helpful to people generally. Hede organised a yoga group, which numbered about twelve when we all were present. I was not part of their exercise group due to my troublesome back. The Polish-American who was in charge of the physical exercises was also a kind, likable man, who I suspect, at a sudden tweak, could dislocate a few more discs in my back. I would occasionally join them for mediation.

One day, Hede phoned me with the exciting news that a Sikh holy man from India was to pay a visit to Quito. I wondered what the attraction could be for him to visit. Maybe the high altitude in the Andes appealed. Perhaps he had been invited by a conscientious follower of yoga. Whatever the reason, a meeting was booked at someone's expense at a very luxurious hotel. Apart from the beautiful pool and well-kept gardens, the biggest attraction to me were the enormous tortoises that enjoyed the freedom of the garden. They were from the Galapagos Islands, situated in the Pacific Ocean which belongs to Ecuador. Bang on the equator, as is Quito.

After the public meeting which had taken place in a large reception area of the hotel, we were privileged to be invited to a private discourse. The time arrived and we were ready.

Shoeless and each clutching a cushion, we quietly filed into the small, unfurnished room. Someone lit a stick of incense, and after a minute or so of deciding where to sit, arranging ourselves into a circle, we were ready. Backs straight, half lotus position for those who could manage it. A few deep breathing exercises, followed by three 'Aum's', and we were away! Meditating or trying to. The end reward being, one hoped, peace of mind! There were quite an assortment of types in that small room. Of the twelve present, only four were males. Ages ranged from twenty to seventy. All of us were fairly new to this particular pursuit of happiness as the 'group idea' had only started three months ago. I suppose we were all drawn to the group for various reasons, apart from the main reason of a search for peace. Whatever it was, one thought united us: to improve our state of mind, and meditation, we were told, was the answer.

I sat cross-legged with them for the entire thirty minutes, not knowing what to think about, or what not to. Having attempted the half lotus position and failed, my main concern during that silent time was how to avoid cramp, which threatened my thigh muscles every other minute. If the spasm finally succeeded, would I be able to resist crying out?

At last, the meditation was over, and everyone tried to rise silently, which wasn't very easy when so many stiffened joints insisted on making a cracking sound. We made our way to the dining hall, led by a cheerful American. The refreshment room buzzed with excited anticipation about the holy man, until the leader of the group, the beaming American, raised his hand for silence. The buzz subsided to a hum.

"In one hour, my friends," he announced triumphantly, "we will go to the main hall for the master's discourse. There will be a short meditation with him, and of course you all know that afterwards, we have been given the special privilege of a private audience with our blessed master.

The excited buzz started up again as I groaned inwardly. More meditation meant the threat of cramp again. Well, I would kneel this time.

At Hede's anxious insistence, we arrived at the hall ten minutes early and made our way to the very front row of seats. Hede was determined to miss nothing. In front of us was a crudely made wooden stage, upon which had been placed a short-legged table with two small steps leading up to it. The table was covered with a gaudy gold silk cloth. A microphone was being positioned on top of the table by a middle-aged American who appeared to be the chief organiser. He ran to and fro, with a harassed expression on his face, adjusting speakers and the microphone several times over. The spacious hall was beginning to fill rapidly, and as we watched the activity, we were approached by one of the Indian organisers, an elderly man with snow white hair. He told us, with his voice rising to an alarming degree, that we should not be sitting where we were because the seats had been reserved for someone else. "And so," he said, with a repeated upwards sweep of his hands, "would you move now?" Glancing behind us, we saw that the room was packed out. Not one vacant chair was left. We sat tight, refusing to budge, while Hede fixed him with an icy imperious stare. He continued to harangue us for at least another minute, then finally, with a loud clicking of his tongue against his teeth, he went away. We breathed an audible sigh of relief.

No time for any comment, for at that moment the American organiser stepped on to the stage to welcome everyone. He talked for a few minutes about his master's struggle for realisation, which of course he had finally mastered, and of how he had performed certain miracles in the past. He ended the introduction with a description of the holy man's eyes, comparing them to the blue sky. The American, clearly moved by his own speech, blew his nose into a large handkerchief and left the stage in tears, leaving me thinking it was rather curious for an Indian to have blue eyes.

The seconds dragged. Then, there he was, seating himself on the table in the full lotus position. He just sat on the silken cloth gazing at everyone, and everyone gazed back at him. He looked quite old, possibly eighty, with a brown face and a long white beard and hair. His figure was full and round and altogether he strongly resembled a friendly Father Christmas.

After clearing his throat a few times, he proceeded with the short discourse. His English was poor, his tone low and rumbling. It was difficult to know if many understood what was being said, but no matter, he rumbled on until it was time for the meditation. His instructions for this were fairly clear.

"Look into your mind with eyes closed, and find stars. Choose a star and plunge yourself into its centre."

I tried obediently to do just that but failed miserably. I

couldn't find a single star in the darkness of my mind to plunge into. The atmosphere however, aided by the strong aromatic perfume of sandalwood filling the hall, was pleasantly quiet and peaceful, except for the occasional clearing of the throat and the odd belch from the holy man. At one point, he actually spat, completely destroying my concentration. I tried very hard not to think about where the product had landed and considered it a good lesson in thought control. Grateful that we were allowed to remain seated, in comfortable chairs. I wondered what the others were thinking about and if they had found a star to plunge into.

Soon after meditation was over, the group trooped back to the dining room again, this time to queue for an uncomplicated lunch of thick curry soup and chapatis. Everyone, except perhaps me, counted the minutes until it was time for the arranged meeting.

The master's living quarters consisted of a small, modest stone bungalow situated behind the hotel and partially hidden by trees and shrubs. Our cheerful leader knocked at the door, and it was immediately opened by the aggressive Indian we had encountered earlier over the seating problems. We all filed in and sat wherever we could in front of our host. Questions were asked, and the master answered them all amiably, smiling benignly from his chair.

"What is the meaning of life?" one student asked.

"It depends on what you mean by the meaning of life," was the reply.

It seemed to me that he answered all the questions without actually committing himself to any positive statement. I thought cynically that he had the makings of a politician.

After the questions, he leant forwards in his chair and

gazed at each one of us in turn. Each person held their breath as his eyes rested on theirs, waiting, hoping for some sort of happening; a mystical experience, a revelation, colours, levitation, anything. When it came to my turn, I too held my breath, but nothing happened. Just a nice old face, and he did in fact have blue eyes.

I remember very clearly a famous Ecuadorian painter and sculptor, Oswaldo Guayasamin. I got to know him with my husband at several parties we attended. He invited us on a couple of occasions to his home. He was a popular and very sociable man. I didn't get to know him that well but was intrigued by his paintings and the fact that he was already famous for his art. Guayasamin was very concerned about the downtrodden. Most of his paintings reflected this. I was not enamoured by his style of painting, but it seems that most of the art world were. His paintings were mostly of suffering, torture, distortion of faces. Canvas after canvas! I certainly wouldn't care for any one of them to be put on my walls. Apparently, he mellowed in his last few years and concentrated more on flowers and landscapes. Beauty somehow took over and freed him from what was called his 'age of rage'. But it was his obsession with suffering that made him famous. He died in 1999.

I can visualise clearly my time in Ecuador. The plaintive, rather mournful reed pipe music of the Andes. Haunting with a definite air of melancholy. We visited friends who had beautiful colonial haciendas (Spanish-style farmhouses.) They conjured up the atmosphere of old colonial life. I enjoyed it all from a visual point of view, however I still preferred my time in the Punjab. I was more content with life. No reason! Just state of mind at that particular time.

Without doubt the most dramatic event during my stay in Quito was an air crash in which my husband was involved. It happened on Tuesday, 7 March 1972. A Cessna 337 Super Skymaster was chartered by Anglo Oriente for a flight from Quito to the Oriente, to take personnel and equipment to Cononaco. My husband wrote the following accident report and because he was in the co-pilot's seat and held a UK pilot's licence, it made him far more qualified to relate professionally the following report on that fateful return flight in detail.

It was at a friend's dinner party when we received a telephone message from Guayaquil airport to say that my husband's plane had crashed on their way back from Quito. They had not yet located where in fact it had crashed.

I felt strongly that no harm had come to the pilot or passengers and then slipped effortlessly into that numbed shock state that I'm particularly good at.

Richard was in the co-pilot's seat with the pilot doctor Marco Ordonez in command. This is part of my husband's report:

After delays on account of bad weather reports, and after flying through atrocious weather and severe turbulence (at one time undercurrents were lifting the aircraft at a rate of 1,000 ft a minute, in spite of attempts to descend) the plane finally reached Cononaco. At 16.25, the aircraft was boarded at Cononaco for the return flight to Quito. Conditions for take-off were good and the course was set for the sierra at 330°, the aircraft climbing in clear skies.

At 16,500 ft the pilot levelled off. Oxygen masks were distributed and oxygen switched on.

The plane carried a pilot and five passengers, and being turbocharged, has good altitude performance, although unpressurised.

As the aircraft approached the sierra, it was seen that, contrary to the weather report received earlier, high, dense black clouds had built up over the Quito area but that the skies were clear and sunny to the north. It was therefore decided to cross the eastern Cordillera of the Andes north of Mount Cayambe, before turning south down the central valley of Quito. On turning south, the weather deteriorated further, and with no VOR signal, it was thus impossible to determine the aircraft's position from instruments alone. Radio contact with Quito was established and a report of bad weather conditions with heavy rain and low clouds was received. After tracking to the south for a few minutes and being unable to locate Cayambe, the captain decided to divert to Guayaquil, since he was faced with a combination of poor instrumentation and bad weather. He began a steep climb to 18,000 ft, hoping to avoid Mount Cayambe at 19,000 ft. The oxygen supply ran out and masks were removed. Position now was uncertain and descent had begun. The ADF equipment was tuned to Santo Domingo, but no signal was received. Continuing to fly on the ADF, the town of Quevedo was overflown at 12,000 ft. The ADF was switched to Quayagil. Light was now failing and bad weather was seen to the south. Soon after passing Quevedo, the aircraft again entered cumulonimbus cloud, which although not very turbulent, produced continuous lightning, which passed on all sides of the aircraft. The rear engine faltered and failed, but power was regained by the captain switching this engine to the north fuel tank. Both engines were then running on this tank.

Descent was continued through cloud, and cabin and panel lights were switched on. It was too dark to read the flight instruments. Lightning was very severe. The aircraft finally descended through cloud base, at about 3,000 ft, some miles north of Quayagil. Scattered lights of various isolated villages could be seen. The captain was in contact with Quayagil Tower by radio and the aircraft was passing through 2,000 ft with the lights of Quayagil just visible ahead, when both engines began to falter. The right fuel indicator was then reading empty, while the left one showed some twelve gallons remaining. The captain tried to regain power by switching tanks, adjusting mixture controls etc, but to no avail. The aircraft began to descend rapidly. As it was now nearly 7pm and dark, little could be seen on the ground, except a glimmer of the Guayas River, some two miles to the west. The pilot turned in this direction and made towards the river, at the same time reporting to Quayagil Tower that he was making an emergency descent after engine failure.

With full flaps, undercarriage retracted and, switching off the aircraft, it touched down at 60mph, skidding rapidly across the wet, swampy terrain, until being brought to a halt on striking a low bank and a small wooden house. The occupants of the aircraft, although thrown forwards, were unhurt, with the exception of my husband, who received a light blow to the chest. Subsequent X-rays revealed some dislocated ribs but nothing broken.

The passengers rapidly evacuated the aircraft, finding themselves in two feet of water and mud in the midst of the wood and planks brought down from the small house. The pilot remained in the cockpit, attempting to advise Guayaquil by radio that the aircraft had safely touched down without injury to the occupants. Unfortunately, he was unable to raise Guayaquil and, after some minutes, was persuaded to leave the aircraft. In the dark, it was impossible to see the extent of the damage to the aircraft, but it appeared not to be too serious. The right wing which hit the supporting poles of the small house was torn in one place, and the propellers were bent. A man, possibly the occupant of the house, quickly appeared and was followed by some five to ten others. These men, called montubios in this region, enquired whether anyone knew of the plane's whereabouts and whether the party was armed. As a precaution in view of the remoteness of the location, they received an affirmative to both these questions, although this was factually incorrect.

T here was naturally considerable anxiety that news of the safe landing should be passed to Quayagil, but this was impossible with there being no telephone in the area. After a few suggestions as to how to get through the mud – it was too tough to make a start on foot – they finally rounded up five horses, two to a horse. Each occupant of the aircraft was accompanied by a montubio guide. The horses were ridden for about an hour in conditions that were so wet and swampy *that at times the horses were practically swimming. Eventually, a mill was reached, and an armed guard delayed the party at its gates until permission to enter could be obtained from the owner. At the mill, a truck was organised, which was driven to the bridge over the Guayas River on the outskirts of Guayaquil. Here, the party was met by the aircraft's owners and news of safe arrival was passed to Guayaquil and Quito.*

Whatever the cause of the accident, there is no doubt that the captain, Doctor Marco Ordoñez, behaved in a very cool, competent and correct manner when faced with a very dangerous situation. And it is in large measure due to his personal skill that the passengers came through the experience unharmed.

Before I leave Ecuador, I feel I should mention the fact one can visit a place near Quito where you can have one foot in the northern hemisphere and the other foot in the southern hemisphere. Tourists love this! It attracts people like us, and we of course had our photos taken to prove it. I wondered how accurate the actual location was.

EVE'S INCENSE

I saw a great deal of Eve and Hede during my time in Quito, but there was one special occasion that I will relate. Eve used to visit Hede's house frequently for meditation and exercises with a small group of women. As I've mentioned before, I did not take part in either due to my back still giving me problems, and I didn't approve of the yoga method of clearing the mind!

Hede called me on the telephone and invited me over for coffee. Her voice sounded unusually excited. Eve was there when I arrived. I settled with my coffee and biscuit, anxious to hear Eve's story. It went as follows. Eve proceeded, "After our group's meditation came to an end, I remained for a short while with my eyes closed, unmoving, reluctant to break the peaceful atmosphere, and that is when it happened!"

"When what happened?" I interrupted.

Hede put a silencing finger to her lips and Eve continued with her story. "I suddenly felt as if I were being taken out of my body. It was such a wonderful sensation. Then I saw someone standing in front of me bathed in light, to such an extent that I was unable to distinguish the features of his face clearly. I only assumed that it was a he and not a she. At the same time, there was a strong impression of incense all around me, so overpowering that it seemed to carry me further and further away from myself. When I finally opened my eyes, everyone was staring at me in amazement, for they too had experienced the strong aromatic incense which apparently enfolded me."

"I can tell you," Hede added, "one moment nothing," she held out her stretched palms to indicate nothing, "then the room was filled with the most exquisite fragrance. I will never forget it. It was the most incredible experience for all of us."

I remained silent, as I thought of all the possibilities that could conjure up such a perfume. I asked Eve, without wishing to dampen her story, "Could there not be a possibility of an incense stick burning at the time?" I felt slightly ashamed of my sleuth-like attitude to her sincere account.

Hede answered for her. "No, absolutely not. There was not a single stick burning in my room today." Her reply was adamant.

"What about people wearing perfume or incense wafting in from nearby eucalyptus trees?"

"The difference is," Hede explained, "the incense arrived quite suddenly, out of nowhere, and then disappeared the same way. You can't turn perfume off like a tap of water. If someone had been wearing the scent or if it had drifted in from nearby trees or plants, then it would be logical to assume that a little of that scent would linger for a short while, not vanish so abruptly."

I was finally convinced that Eve had in fact experienced something ineffable that day and it was more or less confirmed by the events that unfolded over the next few days. The next occasion was a drinks party given by Eve and Claudio. It was held in their spacious garden, set up with chairs and tables and attractively decorated with lights cascading from trees which lit up the whole garden. There was quite a gathering that evening. Drinks and delicious small eats were offered to the guests on trays by Ecuadorian waiters, who hired themselves out for events such as this. My husband and I were chatting amiably with a small group, which included my friend Jenny and her husband John, Eve and Claudio. Suddenly, Eve announced firmly, "It's here," and it was! A strong fragrance enveloped us out of the blue. It was a mixture of allurement and incense so pure and somehow silent. All in our small group experienced it! Eve spoke again after less than a minute and simply said, "It's gone," and it had completely. It left us wondering where it had suddenly gone and, even more perplexing, from whence it came. I left the party still trying to reason that there must be a logical explanation. A few days later, the phone rang; it was Eve, sounding upset. The incense had manifested itself again, and this time Eve was overwhelmed and a little frightened. "Can we come over to you? It's the cook's day off and I was attempting a casserole when the incense returned."

"Certainly," I replied. "Come over now and have lunch with us."

They lived about five minutes away by car, so about ten minutes later their car pulled up outside our house. Richard went to the gate to greet them and told me afterwards that Eve was still surrounded by the fragrance. It disappeared completely as soon as she entered our house.

I talked to her on the phone about a week ago. We get in touch with one another about once a month. I asked her if she had ever experienced that wonderful incense again. "Never," she replied. We didn't discuss it any further. Eve still lives in Vegas with Delph, her second husband, and they seem very happy!

It is the heart that perceives God and not the reason.

PASCAL

SCOTLAND

Our next posting was Scotland. We chose to live in a small town next to the Clyde, called Helensburgh. It had a good train service, so my husband was able to commute to Glasgow daily. It was the most eventful time and place that we ever lived in, because our son Michael and daughter Shanny both went to Edinburgh University and both met and married their soulmates in Scotland. My grandchildren, which numbered five from the north, have flown the nest. Shanny's offspring live quite near her and now she has four grandchildren. Michael's children are further afield but return home frequently. Going back over thirty-five years, we managed to entice our youngest to return with us when we left Scotland to live once again in Surrey. Wendy was seventeen and had left a few admirers behind to start a new life. In no time, she met Phil. They married and had four children. She lives nearby and that, for me, is a blessing. I have a lasting memory of the weather in Helensburgh. Due to the geographical location, the town gets more than its fair share of rain. All to do with nearby adjacent hills creating and forming an abundant number of clouds daily. I didn't ever find it too cold, thanks, I'm told, to the gulf stream, which benefits the west side of the northern hemisphere. On the many occasions I shopped in Helensburgh, I sometimes saw small groups of elderly women standing on windy street corners, chatting cheerfully and laughing. Neatly dressed and always wearing hats, they sometimes protected themselves with umbrellas. What struck me was their positive attitude. They seemed unperturbed by being buffeted by extreme challenging conditions. With my head lowered against such weather, I would hasten past them to my car parked nearby, feeling a silent admiration for their spirits. The Glaswegians have a dry sense of humour, which appeals to me. They are warm people, kind and friendly. In the past, many have been humiliated by object poverty. Even then, they could still produce their wonderful brand of humour. I believe that a sense of humour and a cheerful disposition is inherited. What a wonderful legacy to hand down and longer lasting than money.

Whilst living in Scotland, we once made a visit to the Orkneys. The month was June 1979. We arrived by boat to snow and sleet. More snow than rain on this occasion. It was miserably cold! The object of the trip was a field excursion of Orkney. Exploring interesting archaeological sites, of which there seemed to be many, combined with geological finds, it made fascinating studies. A wealth of standing stones – why were they ever placed there? Possibly ceremonial reasons, all going back about five thousand years. Same time as Avebury and Stonehenge. Quite a number of stone circles, ancient monuments and settlements, including earth houses. No real dating evidence!

The town of Kirkwall is dominated by the old Cathedral

of St Magnus, founded in 1137. We paid a visit and were duly impressed. It's worth a visit, but I would suggest you delay perhaps until August, in hope of warm weather!

We stayed in Kirkwall where George Mackay Brown, a well-known writer, lived. I visited his house in the hope that he might sign the book written by him. I knocked boldly on the door. No one answered.

A very unforgettable memory for all of my family was acquiring a golden Labrador puppy from Loch Lomond Kennels. My advice to my children went unheeded. I said, "If you see a puppy that is not responsive, not playful, but most of all not approaching you when enticed, well then, don't choose that one. It's probably the runt of the litter." It was, and they chose him. He was named 'Rocky'. He was the most extraordinary dog; that's why he is so memorable. At seven months, he dug his way out of the garden by going under the fence. Once he made it into the big world, there was no stopping him. Even though we tried several well thought-out abortive methods, the world remained his oyster. Off he would go, apparently at full speed. We never actually saw him take off; he was far too clever. Rocky pursued many adventures you would just not believe! He would be seen quite often just coursing along the streets of Helensburgh, visiting various shops, we were told, for helpful handouts.

Occasionally, he would get on the Fitzpatrick bus when too tired to return home. Passengers on the bus used to phone us when they reached home. Full of sympathy, they would warn us how tired Rocky was. We picked him up each time at the nearest bus stop. Thanks to his disc with name and telephone number attached to his collar, we were always relieved to see his appealing face again. He was frequently seen jumping off the pier into the water and then when he'd had enough of that sport, would choose a car whose boot was open, which would then return him, courtesy of the exasperated driver, back to our house. The police knew him well. He was put into a dog pound twice. The police sometimes returned him as he had learnt, when tired of adventure seeking, to actually give himself up by walking into the police station. They were amused by him and knew that he simply could not be contained. He always found a way to freedom. Rocky came south with us and continued seeking adventure. I wonder if he ever missed the strong winds roughing his golden coat, or the friendliness of the police who, when he was especially tired after gallivanting, gave him a saucer of sweet tea before returning him home. The Clyde police were never cross, sometimes stern. They knew Rocky for what he was, a complete maverick. He lacked allegiance but was naturally intelligent. Many people in Helensburgh were vying for the chance of adopting Rocky, probably thinking we were lousy owners and that they could mend his wilful ways. No chance! We loved him too dearly.

We found a lovely house in Surrey and settled quite quickly. The house had a large swimming pool, which pleased Wendy. One day, soon after our move, I was walking around the garden with Richard. We went down to the small orchard at the bottom of the garden and, out of the blue, he said, as he looked back at the house, "I like this house very much. It will see me out! What about you?"

I just shook my head and said, "No, I don't think it will." We didn't pursue the subject.

OIL RIG

I could narrate many events that have occurred over the years. Some happy and some less happy and some downright joyful. Our children's weddings, the birth of our grandchildren! But I choose to remember the sad and anxious memory of our son Michael receiving a blow to the head and being knocked unconscious. It happened when we lived in Scotland and Michael was working during the summer vacation on an oil rig out in the North Sea. Thanks to a burly American driller who spotted the heavy metal object falling from great height, he managed to push Michael to one side so that the blow was more glancing than full on. He was wearing a safety hat, but it still made a hole in it.

I quote from a newspaper:

An injured teenager was flown by helicopter to Teesside airport yesterday from a north sea oil rig. The helicopter could not land at Aberdeen airport because of bad weather, and was diverted to Teesside. Michael Fowle, 19, of Helensburgh near Glasgow, was last night

*said to be fair in Darlington memorial hospital with a
head injury.*

Meanwhile, it was a Sunday, and my roast was well on
the way to being cooked. Richard was dealing with a few
odd jobs that needed attention and Wendy, our youngest
daughter, was sitting at the kitchen table and, for some
unknown reason, was writing Michael's full name over and
over on some blank writing paper. We asked after why she
was doing that. Her reply was she didn't know. In retrospect,
I now think it was a very strange thing for her to do just at
that particular time. She didn't stop until the telephone rang,
informing us of Michael's accident. We dropped everything
and drove to Michael's side. By the time we had arrived, he
had regained consciousness. The surgeon was perplexed
and told us after the examination of the patient that, with
having sustained such an injury, his head should now be low
between his shoulders, such was the impact! We prayed all
the way to the hospital, but I think Wendy's input did the
trick.

Years later, Michael was on holiday in the South of Italy
with his wife and children. One night, Ali, his daughter, fell
on the way home from a teenagers' get together. I'm not sure
of the height that she fell, but she was knocked unconscious.
Ali was taken to hospital and took a worrying amount of
time to recover. I can only begin to imagine how the parents
must have felt whilst keeping vigil at her bedside. Thank God
she made a full recovery.

AVEBURY

Back in England, and another upheaval awaited us. It was to sell the first house we bought together, to enable us to move to Richard's new workplace in Swindon. For me, it was a sad move. It was the one and only time I ever became attached to a house. We moved to Wroughton, then soon after to Lechlade to be near the girls' school. Michael was still boarding in Winchester. I can't remember much about that quiet time, except one occasion when we lived in Wroughton.

One of my very good friends Jenny, whom I first met in Ecuador, was staying with me at my home in Wroughton, near Swindon. Although quite a nervous person, she was a delight to have as a guest. I always enjoyed her stay, but on this occasion, she was noticeably unhappy. Jenny's sense of humour seemed to have deserted her, reason being she was going unwillingly through a divorce instigated by her husband and was led like a lamb to slaughter. She obeyed him in demanding nothing except a very small humble abode. It was on this visit, at a time when my husband's company was having huge problems, that the help of Cyrus Vance was sought. He was then the secretary of state in America. He was also the nation's chief diplomat. As a lawyer, he came over with his wife Grace, and I was asked at very short notice to entertain her for lunch later that afternoon. I had to collect my daughter from school and that could not be cancelled.

Then there was Jenny, in the slough of despond in the middle of a divorce, simply because he wanted to marry his mistress. I thought desperately of how I could entertain Grace successfully. There was in fact, in the time given, little choice. I decided on Avebury, which has never attracted as much notice as Stonehenge. *Never mind*, I thought – it would do nicely. Old enough to impress – 2,000 BC. Late Neolithic. We reached the car park and were soon gazing intently at the unique group of prehistoric monuments in north Wiltshire. My guest's expression was undisguised. She was bored. I have to admit, it was a cold day. A cruel north wind was blowing. Poor Grace looked miserable. *Time for an early lunch*, I thought. So, we entered the nearby building and took our place in the queue, armed with trays for our not-too-exciting lunch. I excused myself, leaving Jenny, who was nearing her maudlin stage after downing her second glass of wine, to entertain Grace Vance. I ran over to the museum, which I reached by going through the churchyard. And there, I bought a small book on Avebury and presented it to my guest. I hoped it might produce a smile, and it did! After, we drove back to collect my girls from school, then on to the hotel where I deposited Grace, not without a feeling of relief. Maybe she was suffering from jetlag. Anyway, it was very short notice.

PLANETS

I have been on this planet for quite a long time and yet know so little about anything. I have no idea how I am able to spin around on this Earth without feeling dizzy. I'm completely unperturbed by the fact that the planet I inhabit is moving at such great speed, as are we all, because I can't fathom it. I have circumnavigated the sun eighty-five times so far, whilst spinning at the same time. Now that's travelling! Our planet Earth is a member of the solar system and countless theories have been expounded as to how it all started. How can one interpret this phenomenon? An impossible challenge for our limited reasoning. It's an audacious attempt for even the brightest mind. Let's start with the moon's origin. I don't believe it's there by chance. The moon is not physically related to Earth. The moon's material has been studied (and that's a fact). Its origin has nothing to do with Earth. The passing star theory suggests that it was material dragged from the sun by the gravitational influence of a passing star. Possibly, the planets in our solar system are doing a sterling job keeping us safe by taking the impact of all kinds of outer space debris. Try as I might, I cannot give evolution the credit for such intelligent tactics. Even if life on this Earth had evolved in the way the textbooks tell us, it couldn't explain its perfect pattern. Everything is arranged and ordered in an intelligent design. Too perfect to have just fallen into place over billions of years! Albert Einstein, who is the greatest scientific mind in history, was once asked at a dinner party whether he was religious. He replied, and I quote:

> "Yes, you can call it that. Try and penetrate with our limited means the secret of nature and you will find that behind all the discernible laws and connections there remains something subtle, intangible and inexplicable veneration for this force, beyond anything we can comprehend in my religion. To that extent I am, in fact, religious. I am a Jew, but I am enthralled by the luminous figure of the Nazarenen. No one can read the gospels without feeling the actual presence of Jesus. His personality pulsates in every word. No myth is filled with such life…"

With due respect to our geologists, how do they in fact calculate time? How do they, and this includes palaeontologists and archaeologists, come up with their estimates? Count the rings around tree trunks? Count the layers of rock strata? That's alright for a few thousand years perhaps but not for millions. It's no good suggesting carbon-14 testing because it is now accepted that the method is not reliable. Last I heard, it was up to 36,000 years, but now they say it's just not a reliable source. Anyway, they (the experts) keep changing their minds about the duration of the past. I am certainly not equipped with any knowledge about the past. I don't know anything about Neanderthals, except that they were a type of primitive man. I doubt that anyone else knows a great deal about them either. I once went on a five-day archaeological course in Somerset. Armed daily with digging and scraping tools to assist with our excavations, we all set off enthusiastically to see what we could dig up. Guess what we found. Sharpened flints all over the place, dozens of them. They must have spent all of their time sharpening flints. The experts call it 'napping'.

I remember very well, at the end of the course, wishing never to see another piece of sharpened flint. Meanwhile, the mysteries of the universe continue to be explored as much through suppositions, without proof, as well as pursuing the arduous scientific route.

Having got that off my chest, I will continue to tell my story of my journey on Earth.

THE CHIMNEY

Our daughter Wendy was in her late teens when she made up her mind to have an 'annoying' mole removed from her back. She finally plucked up the courage and made an appointment at the local hospital. It was one of those very rare occasions that my husband Richard had taken the day off from his work in London, and so he offered to drive us to the hospital. We left Wendy in the capable hands of doctor and nurse, and since we were both rather squeamish, we declined the invitation to stay during the short procedure and went for a walk around the hospital grounds. It was a warm October day, so after our brief exercise we sat for a short while on a small area of grass, close to the hospital. Richard turned to look around him and suddenly stopped, transfixed. He was looking at the hospital's very tall chimney; it seemed to stun him.

"What's the matter?" I asked.

He just shook his head. "Let's move away from that." He nodded towards the chimney. Richard was normally not given to fanciful imagination.

"What's the matter?" I repeated. I looked at him and saw an expression of fear.

"I can't put what I have just experienced into words," he said.

I knew that I shouldn't pursue his reaction so said, hoping to console him, "It's just a chimney, just a passage for smoke." This didn't do anything to help. We returned to our daughter, now minus her 'annoying mole' and returned home. My husband died in that hospital about sixteen months later from cancer of the pancreas and the last thing he saw as he lay on his side was the hospital chimney looming through the window.

ETNA

In May 1983, both radio, television and press gave a fair amount of concentrated news concerning the activity of Mount Etna's volcano. Dramatic pictures of glowing lava pouring relentlessly down the mountainside were shown day after day on our television screens, causing shudders amongst us at the thought of the villages which were being threatened with destruction.

My interest in the famous, or infamous, Etna was also a very personal one, because on the 19th of May, I would not only be seeing the volcano for myself but actually making an ascent to the satellite cone whose eruptions were causing all the alarm.

The reason for this fascinating expedition was that my husband had invited me to accompany him, together with a team of seven male geologists, on a field trip around Sicily. The climax of the trip being Etna volcano, where Dr F. Rigo, the leader and organiser of the party, had managed to obtain special permission to go beyond the official safety barrier.

I wasted no time ploughing excitedly through various colourful tourist books on Sicily and gulped a few times reading about the past deeds of Etna, also known as Mongibello. I reminded myself to take a warm jacket, knowing how cold it could be at higher altitudes, and was firmly warned by my husband to take thick stout walking shoes.

"No sooner said than done." I winked at him, then left the buying of these essential shoes until the day before our departure. I refuse to describe my unfortunate feet but will just explain that I spent an entire afternoon searching, without success, to find strong, comfortable shoes. Finally, I settled for a pair that looked fairly sensible but were without doubt light. Wafer thin was how my husband described them when I proudly produced the salmon pink shoes from my suitcase.

By 8am on the morning of Monday, 16 May, we were all assembled in bright sunshine outside our hotel in Palermo to begin the field trip. A white minibus was waiting for us, and soon everyone was comfortably seated and heading towards Agrigento. As we drove along, Dr Rigo, with his expert knowledge of the area, described and explained the various rock formations. The Sicilian driver seemed to be taking a very keen interest in the whole proceedings, despite the fact that he didn't speak English. It was slightly unnerving for the passengers when he gazed intently in whatever direction Dr Rigo happened to be pointing. Completely blinded by science, I concentrated on the passing scenery of almond trees, citrus groves, endless grape vines and giant cactus plants.

Every few miles, at some particularly interesting formation, Dr Rigo would tell the driver to stop. The geologists, equipped with hammers and magnifying glasses, all jumped out and, having found a suitable patch, proceeded to chip enthusiastically away at the rocks to gather samples. I followed at a safe distance, since I had no great desire to receive brain damage or lose an eye from flying pieces of rock. I occupied myself during these energetic intervals by studying the wide variety of beautiful wild flowers and even took to observing the behaviour of very large ants. I found the climate rather hot and my new shoes were not adjusting to their new owner as well as I would have wished.

We stopped for the night at Agrigento and early the following morning set off to combine archaeology with geology on a tour of amazingly well-preserved Greek temples. I walked a great deal and by now, three large blisters had developed on the heels of my feet. However, I continued to limp, though not too stoically, behind the striding geologists.

Tuesday night was spent at Siracusa, and the next morning we visited an excellent museum. More walking. Two more blisters appeared, which at least distracted me from the other three.

We stayed that night in beautiful Taormina. I awoke early the next morning to the singing of birds and a feeling of excitement. The day was Thursday, 19 May. *I'll write an article about this*, I thought smugly, as the minibus climbed its way slowly up the largest active volcano in Europe and the highest mountain in Sicily (3,300m). The cone of Etna, which is a staggering 40km wide, dominates the entire eastern coast of Sicily.

As we climbed the fertile lower slopes, we saw mile after mile of grape vines and citrus trees stretching out before us. A little higher up, heavy perfume from the eucalyptus trees filled the morning air. In desolate stretches, we passed dark masses of lava which had been active in the past. In-between the beds of lava, lush green trees and foliage grew in abundance, all richly fertilised by the volcanic soil. In some cases, there had been healthy vegetation getting a foothold, only to be destroyed again by a later flow of lava.

The first recorded eruption was said to be in 475 BC. Since then, there have been about 140 eruptions. The most serious being in 1669 when the whole of Catania was demolished. A more recent eruption, causing only light damage, was in 1979.

As we climbed higher, the scent of eucalyptus faded and gave way to the strong acrid smell of sulphur. We reached the solitary police post, and the bus was stopped. Dr Rigo explained our purpose and produced the necessary papers to prove that we had permission to go on. The police checked the document then shrugged their shoulders in a way that seemed to indicate that it was our lives and not theirs which were at risk. A few hundred yards further along, the road suddenly came to an abrupt halt. A recent lava flow had covered the whole area and had partially immersed a nearby building.

I gave an involuntary shiver as we set off on foot towards the black mass of what I hoped was cool lava. A stray dog had followed us from the police post. It stopped, suddenly stiff with tension as we approached the lava. I looked back at the poor creature and thought, *how wise!* I followed the others as they began to climb and clamber over the rough, jagged lava. The sulphur fumes were unpleasantly strong. As I limped and stumbled behind, I couldn't help thinking about a warning I'd read in one of the guidebooks. *Explosions from the craters are unforeseeable.* I was interrupted from my daunting thoughts by shouts from the geologists, who were still bounding ahead. They were saying that the lavas in some places were still very hot. At that moment, I discovered the fact for myself. The heat had permeated the thin soles of my shoes, making me leap up and back a few yards.

"Come on," my husband called, holding out an encouraging hand. He'd jumped with the others to the other side of the hot lava. I stood there like the dog, stiff with tension, just wondering what horrors awaited us further along, and firmly decided that this was as far as I would go.

My husband didn't try very hard to persuade me. I think he had a feeling that one of us ought to be around to see our first grandchild which was due in about six weeks. And so, I gave up at about a hundred yards or so from my goal, for over the next ridge, apparently, one could witness a truly amazing sight. The extraordinary spectacle of dark red molten lava pouring from the crater. Slowly, I climbed down and walked back to the road where the stray dog still stood transfixed, although just managing to wag the stump of its tail at the sight of me. I couldn't get into the bus away from the sulphurous smell because the driver had locked it and joined the party. I wandered towards the lava again, partly in boredom and partly to avoid the unwanted attention of the lonely dog. I sat for a moment on a large piece of lava rock, watching sulphurous smoke rising in the air, until the heat from it forced me to stand. Gusts of hot air from the crater blew over me. The silence around was quite eerie. Occasionally, through the smoke in the distance, I could see orange-tinged lava. I tried not to feel anxious about the others and walked back towards the road. As I paced up and down, the dog followed at my heel, its stumpy tail wagging frantically.

Then, joyfully, I saw the party of geologists appearing over the ridge. They waved their cameras and hammers at me, all grinning triumphantly, elated by their experience.

Oh well! I thought consolingly, as we settled ourselves into our seats for the journey to Catania and the flight to Rome. Perhaps I'll come back when the volcano is less active, and next time I'll bring some really good walking shoes…

My wedding day

My family

Sandoway in Burma
(Left-to-right; Michael, Shanny, me and Burmese nanny.)

CAPRI

One year after our Etna adventure, we were going to the island of Capri. A combination of business and pleasure. It sounds exciting and exotic, but as we set off on our journey, I was not feeling too happy. In fact, it was more anxiety that I felt. Richard had been feeling unwell over the last three days. Not wanting to eat in the evening when he returned from work and, uncharacteristic of him, going to bed early. Added to which, he felt slightly nauseous all the time. I accepted his sick bug explanation and was sure he would be alright by the time we left for Italy. The day of our flight arrived, and he still didn't seem any better. We set off feeling rather glum. Our plane landed at Milan where we waited for our second plane, which would take us to Naples. We had planned to stay two nights there and then on to our destination, Capri. My heart sank at the sight of Richard looking reduced and began to regret having started our journey. I was selfishly disappointed when Richard announced that he would not be eating that evening in the dining room. I dined alone and felt the first of many alarm bells. We decided not to stay two more nights in Naples, but to head off the next morning to Capri. This we did, and by now Richard was beginning to look a little yellow. Since we had both had yellow jaundice in the past, we both agreed that it didn't match the symptoms we had previously experienced. I hoped it was nothing too serious to worry about, but those alarm bells kept ringing.

Our hotel in Capri was luxurious to say the least. There was a very large display of assorted fruits, including black grapes, which cascaded from the overloaded bowl, giving the room an air of decadence. Fruit was in fact the only food that Richard felt remotely any enthusiasm for. Later, we joined the other members of our group, who were assembled in the reception area. My husband was wearing sunglasses in the hope of disguising his problem. It didn't fool his colleagues. He managed to socialise the next day for a short while, but that was it. Richard was seriously unwell. I talked to a very friendly couple in the reception lounge that evening. They were Americans on their second honeymoon. He happened to be a doctor, and when I described how Richard was feeling and looking, he said, without hesitation, "Get him to the mainland and go home immediately." We did just what the doctor advised.

We arrived back in England the next day and went straight to the doctor's surgery, after which he was whisked off to hospital for various checks, which confirmed that he had cancer of the pancreas. Knowing absolutely nothing about the pancreas, we all hoped surgery would solve the problem. It didn't.

Richard died on the 2nd of June 1984. His family were all present at his bedside. The view from his window, probably the last thing he ever saw, was the large chimney looming in full view. The chimney that had upset my husband so much sixteen months before.

My children were brave and, although stoic, they were grief-stricken at the loss of their father, whom they all loved dearly. Being less stoic, I went into shock and stayed that way for some time, all with strong support from my children who helped me endure. Richard's parents were wonderful and supportive. We were all broken-hearted that such a special and wonderful person was taken from us. He was fifty-three years old.

The one and only time I ever sensed Richard's presence was in the early morning. At least five hours after he had died. I was finally asleep and then the clear ringing of a telephone woke me up. It was my subconscious that was doing the ringing, I know that! I answered the telephone and, now wide awake, a familiar voice said simply, "Hello," nothing more. In that one word was Richard's essence, his entire essence. My imagination was not capable of such a trick.

A LETTER FROM MY
FATHER - IN - LAW

(Dick died on the 2nd of June 1984)

3 June 1984

Pat, my dear,

Grandma and I were sitting quietly together last night, and I was reading odd precis from a book last night called The Testament of Man.

Now you may know of the Essenes[1], a religious sect of two thousand years ago whose works, the so called Dead Sea Scrolls, *were found in Qumran[2], just after the last war. The historian Josephus said this of them:*

Their doctrine is this, that bodies are corruptible and the matter they are made of is not permanent;

---

1 Judaism. A member of an ascetic sect that flourished in Palestine from the second century BC to the second century AD, living in strictly organised communities.

2 An archaeological site in NW Jordan, near the NW shore of the dead sea. Includes the caves in which *The Dead Sea Scrolls* were found.

but that the souls are immortal and continue for ever; and that they come out of the most subtle air, and are united to their bodies as to prisons, into which they are drawn by a certain natural enticement, but that when they are set free from the bonds of the flesh, they then, as released from a long bondage, rejoice and mount upward.

Pop.

A few days after Richard's death, the family were gathered at my house. It must have been the day after his funeral. They all decided to go for a walk together. It was the first time I had been left alone. At first, I felt relieved and felt at peace with my solitude, allowing myself a few grieving sounds. But then I was frightened when it developed into uncontrollable mourning which rose in volume. I thought I would never be able to stop the violent grief pouring out. However, I did manage to stem the flow of tears before they returned. It's probably helpful and necessary to allow one's grief to rise to the surface to have its noisy outburst. I used to sniff at people when I lived in the Middle East who indulged in loud wailing when grieving. I don't sniff anymore! I'm still not able to face the unbearable pain of losing Richard. Every single day for two years, I went over and over the final days which led to his passing. I couldn't let go; it wouldn't let go! Then one day, I realised I had not been preoccupied to the exclusion of all else. The day had actually passed without thinking once of Richard. Relief and guilt mingled; I was able to continue with my life. At the very beginning, my children complained about me making strange, unearthly sounds in my sleep. I was completely unaware of this. How little we know of the unconscious mind. I entered the world of widowhood unhappily. It's a very sad state to be in! It was difficult at first but became less so as time moved on. Shock is a great cushion for the mind. When I finally came out of it, everything seemed rather harsh and raw! However, time really does heal!

My first great loss was my father. I adored him! His health was never robust. Made worse by smoking heavily, which resulted in emphysema putting a strain on his heart. He was a brave man but ill-equipped for this world. He was fifty-four years old when he died. My other loss was my grandmother. On reflection, it was only after her death that I realised how good and caring she had been to me.

In my teens, I felt then that the world revolved around me. How selfish I was. Maybe all young people feel like that, in which case I can distribute the guilt and lighten the load.

My mother died in August 1993. My good friend Sister Anne experienced something that is worthy of relating concerning my mother, less than twenty-four hours after she had passed.

SISTER ANNE

One day in August 1993, an unexpected phone call from my half-brother's partner shocked me with the news that my mother was very ill with cancer of the oesophagus. Now, I hardly knew my mother, since from the age of almost six I had lived in Cambridge with my maternal grandmother. My mother was thought to have two or three months left to live! My brother insisted that she be spared the seriousness of her illness and led her to believe that the pain was due to duodenal ulcers. I felt sure that she really knew the truth but went along with his explanation anyway. With an excuse that I was visiting the area, I arranged a visit. The excuse was so as not to alarm her in any way. Sadly, there was no great bonding between us, but I did feel love for my mother, and she was without doubt a very likable person. After spending a couple of hours with her, I said my goodbyes with a heavy heart. At odd moments I had seen her chin wobble and tears filling her eyes, as she told me of her plans to build a bungalow close to her best friend Kathy, but her tears were persistent and belied her optimistic plans for the future.

The next day, I called my close friend Sister Anne Mccoy. She was a Franciscan nun who had nursed Richard during his illness. I told her that my mother had only about three months left to live. Sister Anne said she would pray for her and that she was off to Assisi in Italy the very next day on her annual one-week pilgrimage. A week passed when I received another call from my brother's partner. It was Saturday afternoon. It was to let me know that my mother had died at 12.30pm that day. We talked about dates for the funeral. No one had expected her to die so soon. The call left me deeply saddened but not in shock or with as much sorrow as was felt by my half-brother. He adored her and was simply beside himself with grief.

The following evening, Sunday, at about 10pm, I received a phone call from Sister Anne. She told me that she had just arrived back from Assisi and wanted to tell me that at the 7am mass that very morning (the last day of her pilgrimage), she'd experienced my mother's presence on the right-hand side of her. She emphasised the fact that the presence was very strong indeed. I was confused to say the least, because Anne had never met my mother physically, only a presence, and added that she knew who it was without any doubt. I asked Anne what she thought the reason was for making her presence felt so soon after her death. I explained that my mother died on Saturday at midday. Anne added she was not surprised and that my mother seemed very peaceful. I couldn't understand how less than twenty-four hours after her death, she had visited Sister Anne. Anne explained that when this happens, the sisters feel sure that the deceased want us to pray for them. Anne was capable of deep prayer, which most of us are not. Perhaps then, that was the explanation. Someone she had never met in her life and yet my mother was able to make her presence felt. It's beyond my comprehension!

Sister Anne died some years ago, having suffered great pain towards the end. It seems necessary for many of us to suffer in some way regardless of whether we are good or bad. I can't expound on this subject since I don't even begin to understand it.

ISRAEL

About twenty years ago, I went on a pilgrimage to the Holy Land in Israel. It was with a catholic group which included my good friend Sister Anne. From the airport in Tel Aviv, we were taken by coach to Bethlehem, where we stayed for three days in a Christian-run hotel. I awoke the next morning and drew back the curtains to reveal a white world outside. At first, I thought it must have been caused by a sandstorm, but no, it was definitely snow. Only a thin covering, but enough to look strangely out of place. I had never imagined Bethlehem in snow, even though a few Christian cards depicted unrealistic winter scenes. After breakfast, the snow turned to sleet and then later that day, to rain. We all felt miserably cold as we set off to visit the Basilica of the nativity and then on to a well-run orphanage, where Christian volunteers took turns throughout the year in helping to care for the orphans of varying ages. Most of us had packed light clothes, suitable for warmish weather. Served us right for not doing our homework on Israel's weather. The month was February. I can now tell you first-hand that it does very occasionally snow in Bethlehem. The next day we visited Jerusalem, only five miles away. I remember walking up and down the Via Dolorosa several times. Our guide, who was a Catholic priest from Africa, was an absolute character. Full of humour, we all envied his energy. He accompanied us throughout the whole pilgrimage, never giving us time to saunter, more keeping us at a brisk pace. In Jerusalem, he led us around all the different quarters – Christian, Moslem, Armenian, Jewish – ending up at the old city to see the dome of the rock and the wailing wall. Finally, we went to the place of the holy sepulchre, and I have to admit that by now I was totally confused, that is confused in which order I had seen everything. It was too much in too short a time. A visit to the garden tomb was the end of the day's pilgrimage. Our African priest celebrated mass in the garden of Gethsemane. It restored our peace and was very memorable.

During the following days of our pilgrimage, we visited Khirbet Qumran. We only saw the caves but didn't enter any. The caves in which *The Dead Sea Scrolls* were discovered were found by a young shepherd, looking for a warm place to shelter whilst tending his sheep. On my next visit to Jerusalem, I went to a museum where the scrolls were on display. What patience, what dedication required to assemble the tiny fragments of writing, and in doing so, make sense of them. What a labour of love. Géza Vermes, a Hebrew bible scholar, translated *The Dead Sea Scrolls* into English to enable us to read about them.

We continued our pilgrimage, visiting all of Israel. We went on a boat in the sea of Galilee, and there I read the gospel, after which I became a regular reader for the group. We were invited to a meal in Cana, then stopped at Nazareth for the night. At some stage, we visited the Dead Sea but did not go into the water because we were told it was unsafe due to political unrest at the time we were there. I could never understand why so many people in the world seem united in being so against the Jews. They are without doubt a gifted race. Is it envy, then? Whatever evil (and it does exist) works hard to turn people against them? Is there any other explanation? People seem to be completely blocked from analysing why the world is against them. No reason! Hate stems directly from evil, which is the complete opposite of love!

We visited a museum dedicated to the victims of the Holocaust. I declined, since I didn't want to live the memory of the unspeakable destruction of life again. I had already taken that horror of events on board long ago.

At some time during our pilgrimage, we walked along a path opposite the not-too-steep hill, where Our Lord had delivered his sermon on the mount! To see all these places with familiar names was wonderful. To walk in the footsteps of Jesus made it all so special and unforgettable.

NO BRAKE FLUID!

continued to travel the world to see new places, make new friends, but there was no denying it. The light had gone out for me since Richard died, and nothing or no one on Earth could ever replace it. That doesn't mean that I am permanently miserable or sad. I'm not! I was and still am game to run the course. I've only been depressed on one single day of my entire life. Many years ago, when the children were very young, I set off to collect my husband from the airport. I was driving an XKI40 Jaguar, my husband's favourite toy. I took my children and my father, who was recovering from a long illness and was still very frail. He lived with me at the time. They were packed like sardines in the car, there being so little space. Richard had been away for three long months in Ecuador, South America. Therefore, it was great excitement for us all. The flight was delayed by an hour or so, and so was Richard. He was hauled off to a customs office, and there they gave him a thorough search! For some reason or no reason, they must have suspected him of concealing drugs or something, or just picked him out at random! Angry and humiliated, Richard finally emerged from the exit of 'nothing to declare'. It definitely spoilt our happy reunion. Driving in silence and my father almost expiring with the three children sitting on top of him, we finally reached the top of the steep hill leading to our house in Woking. At this point, I stopped the car and asked Richard to drive the rest of the way, which was a short distance of about a hundred yards downhill.

"Why?" he asked.

"Because the car has no brakes at all!"

He looked at me disbelievingly. It was true! The brake fluid had somehow all leaked out. I think that was the final straw for poor Richard's jet-lagged brain. He could not understand how I was able to drive under such conditions without incurring some serious accident. I couldn't fathom it either!

It was the next day that I experienced my one and only depression. I'm glad I did so that I can understand what others with the same problem are going through. I walked in slow motion, and my mind became locked in a miserable black cloud. In an attempt to cheer me up, Richard took me out for an Indian curry that evening. Driving on the way home, the depression began to magically lift and then left me completely. It happened quite suddenly, and I thanked God for the return to normal. Just one day, and I know now that you can't just tell someone with a similar problem to pull themselves together. Was it caused by an overload of too much adrenaline the day before, due to a combination of Richard's return and driving hazardously with no brakes?

THE ELECTRICIAN

15 December 2004

I can tell this story only because of the sequence of events that followed. It's a story that cannot just be my imagination, simply because of how and when it happened. I'll start from the beginning. In March 2004, I moved from a house in Guildford to an apartment in Haslemere, Surrey. It seemed just right for me but in need of a fair amount of updating. Over the next nine months, I had two new bathrooms installed, improvements to the kitchen and decorated throughout. By December, it was almost complete. There was just one more job to be done. It was to install an air vent in the bathroom of the main bedroom, which I was told required a qualified electrician.

On the morning of the 15th of December 2004, the electrician duly arrived an hour earlier than expected. I led the way to the bathroom then bustled off to make a cup of coffee. Having delivered it to him, I returned to the kitchen, where I donned my seldom worn rubber gloves to busy myself at the sink, washing pots and pans that were not suitable for the dishwasher. After what seemed like a very short time, the electrician called out to me from the bathroom, announcing that he had finished and was leaving. I asked if he wanted to be paid. He replied that his boss would sort it out and send a bill. I stood in the doorway of the hall, still wearing the rubber gloves and waved goodbye to him as he went off down the narrow hall to the door. I then returned to the kitchen and immediately plunged my hands into the soapy suds again. I had no sooner done this when it seemed the electrician had suddenly returned and was standing behind me. He said, and these were his very words, "I just want to make you aware, to beware of this. Don't touch it." As he spoke, his hand circled the electric dishwasher switch on the wall, which was in front of me to the right. I didn't turn around to look at him whilst he was speaking. It seemed to happen all so quickly. I just stared at the switch uncomprehendingly and then he was gone. My hands were still immersed in the soapy suds. I really didn't understand what he had been warning me about, but I did wonder what on earth the kitchen switches had to do with the bathroom, which was some distance away across the hall.

I made a mental note to phone the electrical shop later to ask him to explain, however, I put it to the back of my mind and went out for lunch. The day passed and I hadn't phoned. That evening, as I watched television, I was suddenly aware that the kitchen lights had gone off and the dishwasher had stopped mid-cycle. I checked the electric box in the hall to see if anything had tripped. It hadn't. Back in the kitchen, I stared again at the switch, remembering what the electrician had said to me. Then the lights came on again and so did the dishwasher. I sat down to watch television and after a few minutes, the lights then went off again in the kitchen and so did the dishwasher, for a second time. Remembering the electrician's warning, I did not touch anything and resolved not to do so until I had phoned the electrical shop. Early the next morning, I phoned the 'boss' and told him about the problem. He said he would come over himself during the morning but was perplexed to hear that the kitchen light went out at the same time as the dishwasher, since they were in no way connected. I then told him how the electrician had warned me and that I did not understand what he had been saying. The 'boss' said, "The electrician is in the shop at the moment, perhaps you had better have a word with him."

I started with, "Remember when you warned me yesterday morning not to touch and beware of the switch behind the dishwasher—"

He interrupted me, saying, "I'm sorry, madam, I don't know what you are talking about. I didn't go into your kitchen or anywhere near it. I only dealt with your ensuite bathroom."

There was silence and I felt my hair stand on end. I muttered that I would wait for Steve (the boss) to come and sort it all out. Steve arrived shortly after and began explaining that the ceiling lights were nothing to do with the wall switches. He said, "Totally unconnected, had to be a complete coincidence." Then he asked me to explain what had happened.

I replied, "I'll tell you about it after you've checked the problem."

Steve disconnected the electricity and unscrewed the switch which the mysterious hand had circled. He shook his head in disbelief as he held the part in his hand and showed it to me. It was damp and rotten, with some broken wires. I asked him if my life could have been in danger. All he said was, and this he repeated several times, "My God, all I can say is that you must have a good guardian angel."

When I told my friends and family this account, they all asked why I didn't turn around to look at whoever was in my kitchen warning me. I was too intent in those few seconds, trying to understand what on earth he was talking about, and I assumed it was the voice of the electrician. I was too focused on staring at the switch on the wall; then he was gone. For whatever reason, I did not question the strangeness of this. I was told that if I had touched the switch or machine with wet hands, then I might not have been around to write this account.

LAS VEGAS

Until about eight years ago, I went every year in the month of November to Las Vegas. Not to gamble, as you might imagine, but to visit my English girlfriend Eve and her Italian husband Claudio. I first met them in Ecuador, South America. He was then manager for Bank of America. When he retired, they moved from LA to Las Vegas. Reason being the cost of living was much cheaper there. That is, as long as you don't gamble, and neither did. I found the climate there far too hot for comfort. I limited my visits to Christmas shopping only, which I did for my nine grandchildren. I stopped this ritual when Claudio died and Eve married a very likeable man, Delph. I attended their wedding. Eve, as always on special occasions, looked stunning. She had in the distant past been a successful model and had small acting parts in quite a few films. Delph is now ninety-three and Eve has reached eighty. Both are still active in Las Vegas. Las Vegas means 'the meadows' in Spanish. Wishful thinking, I feel! It needed very serious irrigation and still does. Right now, it is suffering from severe drought. No rainfall for over two years and not too sure about their water supply in the future. Still, it's an amazing place! Apparently, you can see its lights from outer space! The first wedding I went to was at the famous 'Little White Chapel' in Vegas, to see Hede, my Austrian friend, and her ex-husband Rudi, get remarried. For tax reasons, I was told! No sign of the holy sacrament, but someone who looked awfully like Elvis Presley was present!

DURANGO

Not long after they were married, I joined Eve and Delph on a nine-hour car journey to Durango, in Colorado. I found it all fascinating. We passed a few native American reserves. I want to call them colonies, but they are not, because they were there first! Delph did all the driving and incidentally, I marvelled at the fact and was grateful that he didn't fall asleep on route. Durango is a small, well-run town, which is mostly geared for tourists. I found the whole town neat and very appealing. Delph had a farmhouse, which had a long drive. At the entrance were railway tracks, which were still in operation. A train occasionally chugged by, and as it neared the town, which was close to the farmhouse, it made a sound just like it did in the old cowboy films. Its long, plaintive whistle brought back memories of my childhood, when my imagination would contribute to the sounds emanating from the large screens of the cinemas. I didn't know that the nostalgic whistle had stayed so firmly in my memory. I liked Durango and felt the long journey had been well worthwhile. The second morning of my stay, I came down to the kitchen and observed, not without some trepidation, a huge bear's paw imprint on the outside window. It made me shudder, but I was told by my hosts that the poor creature was not trying to gain entrance into the house but simply trying to get at the sugar water which was placed near the window in a ceramic container for the tiny hummingbirds. I personally would have removed the sugar water to a safer distance, further away from the windows. But then, I am by nature overcautious about most things and certainly lack a sense of adventure generally. If I had to ford a river in my youth, I would search for the shallowest part to cross. If I climbed trees, I would check over and over the strength of its branches.

Quite a few years before visiting Durango, I had gone with Eve and Claudio on a five-day trip to Sedona in Arizona. A similar set up, but not as appealing or attractive. They concentrated too much on tarot cards and other occult nonsense. We paid a visit to the Indian Hopi reservation. We gazed for a time at them hopping up and down with a distinct lack of enthusiasm. They moved slowly around a large circle, all with vacant expressions. I felt sorry for them and wished I could cheer them up, or at least oversee fair distribution of money collected by the native Indian organiser from tourists. He was dressed, to put it mildly, in expensive attire, in sharp contrast to his performing circle. On both journeys to Arizona and Colorado, I was amazed at the interesting rock formation. Everything is on a huge scale compared to our small, compact island.

BACK PROBLEM

Soon after the birth of my first child Michael, I suffered painful back problems. It didn't improve as the years passed. I did consult a specialist once and was told that due to a curvature of the spine, my discs were popping out one by one. This doesn't sound like a very professional description of my then medical condition, but my pain wasn't fussy about how it was described. I continued to live with the problem, helped by wearing a metal corset for quite a few years. The second specialist I consulted suggested ball bearings to replace my discs. He said with some optimism that it could be done in Sweden. Apparently not available in England at that time. I declined politely and said I would give it some thought!

By now we were in Quito, Ecuador and had taken up residence in our first rented house. It was unusual in that it was surrounded by a moat and the house itself was arranged upside down. That is, we slept downstairs whilst the sitting and dining areas were situated upstairs. One soon got used to it, although I still preferred the regular set up.

One morning, I went upstairs to have my breakfast. Our help consisted of two female cousins who all too often seemed offhand and sarcastic. Maybe it was just as well that my Spanish was limited. I remember that I had a boiled egg and coffee. They went in and out of the kitchen's swinging door, making the simple breakfast look like a Labour of Hercules. One asked, with a glance and a grin in the direction of her cousin, if I felt any pain. I just shook my head! I got up and walked, almost doubled since I was unable to straighten up due to stiffness, until about midday. As I walked towards the stairs, I felt resentment and anger towards the two women. I prayed as I walked away from them. If my back was not to be healed, then so be it! But, I asked, could I please keep my sense of humour and not feel resentment. I continued downstairs. I was meeting my friends Jenny and Olga for lunch. I had a shower, dressed and waited for them to arrive. The day passed like any other, helped by my metal corset which gave me confidence in movement.

The next morning, I awoke – no stiffness; no pain! To this day, I have never felt that pain again caused by slipped discs, arthritis? I was able to dispose of my metal corset. Back in England, my doctor told me that my curvature of the spine was now completely straight, a thing of the past.

Thank God!

WISHING AWAY TIME!

I seem to remember clearly the experiences that had a significant 'otherness' about them. Many years ago, I was busy preparing lunch for my young children. On this day, my sense of humour seemed to have deserted me, which was unusual, since I had always depended on it to see me through all eventualities. I don't know why I was so edgy that day. It's possibly why I remember it so well! The children were perched on high stools at the breakfast bar, legs were swinging as they waited. It was a mistake to assemble them whilst I was cooking! They quickly became tired of waiting and began to tickle each other, which turned to pinching, accompanied by shrieks and loud protests. As I fried the fish on the hot stove, the fat added to my irritation in that it occasionally spattered up into my face. I backed away with annoyance, my nerves frayed and on edge. Each time I approached the pan again, it was with caution. Prodding the fish, I reflected on how many meals I had prepared in the past and wondered how many times in the future I would stand at my stove in this frame of mind. It was definitely not a good day for me. There I was, feeling irritable, tired, and much worse, constantly wishing away time.

I was suddenly reminded of a well-known psychologist's theory, which I had just read about. It was that the whole human race is entirely controlled by its environment. That we are all mindless and without free will. I dispute that very strongly! I believe that we are all given free will, in other words, free choices. I thought the psychologist's assumption rather harsh. He added that laughter is genetic, meaning we inherit a sense of humour rather than develop one. I couldn't bear the thought that miserable dispositions were inherited. The very idea saddened me. However, now with hindsight, I tend to go with his theory but not the 'without free will' part.

As I served the food onto warmed plates, I prayed silently for help to live in the present. *Stop me wishing their childhood away*, I pleaded. In that same instant, something happened to me. The kitchen seemed to have taken a rosy glow, and a strange stillness pervaded the kitchen. For the first time in my life, I felt completely at peace and indescribably happy. For a brief moment, time had actually stood still. No beginning; no end. I tried hard to hold onto that timeless state but couldn't. However, it made me aware and I vowed I would at least try and live in the present, and sometimes, I almost succeeded. As for love, it was always there and always will be. Amidst the bored shrieks, spitting hot fish pans and bad hair days, love never left for a single second.

PARTING GIFT

This is a very sad memory of my father's death. He had telephoned just after lunch, as I had requested, to tell me about his appointment with the chest specialist that morning. "Hopeless waste of time," he grumbled. He sighed, which he did a great deal because he lacked energy and oxygen. "Anyway," he continued, "they can't do anything for me. Can't cure my condition, so no reason to make any more appointments. I can do without being lectured like a naughty child."

I didn't know what to say. He was diagnosed with emphysema at only fifty years of age. To be fair, the doctor's remarks were valid. My father was a heavy, long-time smoker, hence the reason for his problem. It was the 1st of November and usually cold. The bitter weather just made his breathing worse. About two months before he had fallen down the stairs and broken several ribs. "Does it hurt?" I'd asked over the phone at the time.

"Only when I breathe," was his reply!

As a child, I had always adored my father. He was my hero, and I thought he was absolutely perfect. When I reached my teens, I still adored him but realised that he was less than perfect, and his pedestal had begun to wobble a little. Meanwhile, my grandmother, who was quite old by then, continued living alone. Her only concern seemed to be caring for everyone but herself. Mid-afternoon, the phone rang. It was John, a friend of my father's. He lived in the same apartment block by courtesy of his sister, who owned the whole building. "Your father asked me to phone you to let you know that he is feeling unwell, and he would like to see you."

"What do you mean, he's not well?" I asked. "Has he seen a doctor?" "No, not yet. He thinks it's his usual bronchitis."

I thanked him for letting me know and explained that I couldn't visit him until the weekend. I asked if he could call the doctor to see my father today. John promised he would and replaced the receiver. Late that same evening, my husband managed to get through to the doctor, who confirmed that he had indeed visited his patient. "No need to panic," he'd said. It was bronchitis. Nothing that medicine couldn't put right. We received that news with great relief! My father had stayed with us for some months after his last illness and left late summer with the promise that he would return when the weather turned cold. He was a stubborn, independent man. Maybe I left out proud! He came and went as he wanted to.

It was sometime before seven the following morning, which was All Souls' Day. The phone rang. It was John with the sad news that Dad had died during the night. He found him in bed, propped up with two pillows for support. He said there was an unmistakable smile on his peaceful face. Whilst Richard was downstairs talking to John, and before he had told me the sad news, I shared a little of that peace in my bedroom, a parting gift. Just for a minute or so. He was fifty-four years of age! Later, I looked out of the window at the cold, frosty morning and, as grief set in, wondered where my father was. Where had he gone?

It is no great thing to live long nor even to live forever, but it is a great thing to live well.

ST AUGUSTINE OF HIPPO

DOT OF LIGHT

Many years ago, we were back in England for a few weeks on a break from Ecuador. During that time, my close friend visited me with her husband and two daughters. My husband had gone off somewhere abroad on a business trip for a few days, so I was on my own with the children. My friend and her family were staying overnight, which was a bit of an upheaval but manageable! My sister-in-law, who lived nearby, had the girls for the night, and my son Michael stayed with Andy, his friend. I spent that night in the girls' room in the lower bunk bed. I remember waiting for sleep, when I was suddenly aware of a tiny bright light way off in the distance. I blinked several times, then opened my eyes wide. Closed or open, the tiny light was still there, and I was certainly not asleep. The dot of light journeyed towards me, travelling like a meteor. It flooded my head and then my whole being. The light then receded again to a dot in the distance. The light did this twice more. Flooding over me, then receding to a dot of light. I lay still in the darkness for a long time, waiting and hoping for the light to appear again, but it didn't. I have no idea what it meant or why it had happened. To describe it, well, the nearest attempt would be a kind of spiritual embrace. Not long after, I returned to Ecuador. I experienced it once more. This time, it flooded over me just once. I still don't know why. I accept it as another gift!

PADRE PIO

I attended a Catholic school from the age of twelve and was fortunate enough to have had a teacher who introduced me to the lives of the saints. I found them all fascinating and enjoyed reading about their paths to sainthood. I must say that I was never envious of their lives, which involved so much suffering. I could never understand the necessity! I didn't get it when reading about them, and I still don't get it now! I felt that Our Lord would not want such suffering. But there it is! Pain is a mystery. Such souls must be chosen for a very special reason! I think they are chosen rather than choose. They also experienced, whilst on Earth, something so wonderful that more than compensates for the pain involved during their tribulations.

My favourite saints are Padre Pio and St Teresa of Ávila. I'll write about the former saint because he's a great part of my past, in that his life captivated me when he was alive and still does even though he died in 1968.

Padre Pio lived in the small town of San Giovanni Rotondo, but he was born in Pietrelcina, a village in the province of Benevento. His real name was Francesco

Forgione. He was the fourth child born into a poor family on the 25th of May 1887. Certainly not well off! Dirt floors, tiny window. Like most saints, no hint of luxury. He was the only ordained priest to ever have received the stigmata, which consisted of a deep gash in his side and perforations in his hands and feet, which, at certain frequent times, bled effusively. He suffered constant excruciating pain for over fifty years. He bore the stigmata for all those years. Death must have been very welcome. Incidentally, his wounds completely disappeared two days before his death. No scars, no marks whatsoever. Doctors and scientists – which numbered many – had in the past examined him, but all were unable to give any explanation. The poor man spent most of his life hidden away from the outside world. He was best known for hearing confessions and knowing what was in the penitent's heart, before they had even entered the confessional. There were some authenticated accounts of his being able to be in two places at the same time. Bilocation it's called! One account in particular I remember reading about involved a businessman living in Scotland. He was going through an anxious time. I imagine it was to do with money! He apparently had known Padre Pio quite well in the past and had written to him for his advice. On this occasion, the man was sitting in his drawing room discussing his problems with his wife, when suddenly Padre Pio appeared to them in the room, and according to them both, very much in the flesh. He talked with the businessman for a short while, then just disappeared into the air, leaving the man relaxed and far less anxious about his problems. At the time that the meeting took place in Scotland, witnesses confirmed that the priest was also very much in the flesh residing in his small cell in a remote part of Italy. The BBC actually interviewed that businessman in 1968, soon after Padre Pio's death. Interesting to know that the man's material problems got through to the priest's compassion. Pio's favourite saying, which is quoted all over the world, is 'pray, hope, and don't worry'.

ST TERESA OF ÁVILA

I admire St Teresa for many reasons. A saint who had achieved so much in her sometimes-tortured life. She was positive, gutsy, fun, loving, with a good sense of humour. At times she became very ill and worse, depressed. Teresa was a Carmelite nun. There was a time when Teresa was not in a hurry to become a nun. Part of her was conscientious and a true religious, but the other part was flippant, with her feet firmly fixed in this world. She travelled frequently around Spain, establishing new convents and new orders, which was not easy in the sixteenth century. She searched for God, and soon found that spiritual love. 'Seek and you will find'. The greatest of her attributes was her writing. I think she wrote about four books, poetry and many letters. Teresa was an intellectual. I believe she was very close to God. A truly remarkable woman! She occasionally came up against the dreaded inquisition, which was rife at the time and possibly more dangerous for Teresa because her paternal grandfather was Jewish and continued to practise his faith. The objection to Judaism and the Islamic faith is that they don't accept the holy trinity as being so. Whatever, Christians often ignore the fact that God has given us all free will. Even in good faith, no one has the right to take this free will away!

> *Remember the sinner who is sorry for his sins is closer*
> *to God than the just man who boasts of his good works.*
>
> ST PIO OF PIETRELCINA (1887–1968)

FAITH

Many times in the past, I have attempted to contemplate on the meaning of life. I imagine most of us have! I'm constantly blocked by my reasoning, which cannot fathom why it is necessary for some poor souls to endure pain, where for others they seem to get off lightly. Good people suffer, including innocent children. It brings me to the suffering of saints: why does one have to undergo this pain more than another and yet carry an equal amount of sin to atone for? It doesn't seem fair to a finite mind. I have the same problem with original sin. Adam and Eve being the forerunners. I'm just not getting the picture! It was such a long time ago! There is so much we really don't understand, and people throughout the ages have tried to explain, forgetting to add that it's God's way of thinking and not ours! So far, I have been one of the fortunate! In that I had a wonderful husband; I have wonderful children and nine wonderful grandchildren.

Grandchildren are the crowning glory of grandparents.

PROVERBS 17:6

I have four great grandchildren, soon to be six! In all, an absolute blessing, and yes, I do remember at times to thank God for them. Difficult not to be earthbound though, when one is steeped in the many enticements of this world. However, it is easier to attempt when one is old. Many experiences have occurred; many mistakes have been made. Now is a time for reflection. After my religious experience at eighteen, I tried for a while to be concerned mainly with the desire of eternal matters. I didn't pursue this narrow path for long. Too many distractions!

What's the use of a long life, when we show so little improvement? Long life unfortunately does not always improve us, but often piles up sins instead.

THOMAS À KEMPIS (1380-1471)

I don't think we should let sadness take over, because I believe that in doing so it prevents our being filled with the holy spirit.

George Orwell once said 'that man can only be happy when they do not assume that the object of life is happiness'.

However, without being at variance with George, I don't think that we are predisposed to misery but only to joy, which is all too often pushed to one side by sin. I would make a very poor apologetic because I find it difficult to remain calm in certain discussions. I feel I could do more harm than good at advocating the Christian cause. But I do know that joy can suddenly arrive and not always be deserved but simply a gift.

Atheists often get angry when they discuss God who, for them, does not exist. Why so angry if he isn't real? Think carefully about this next sentence.

If there were no God, there would be no Atheists.

G.K. CHESTERTON (1874–1936)

We can think and try to reason for the rest of our lives, but we will never know all the answers. If we did, and all our questions were explained, it would take away our free will of faith. Take away the freedom of choice, which has been given to us.

It is the heart which perceives God, not the reason. That is what faith is. When questioned, many people say, 'just go with the flow'. Well, don't. Only dead things go with the flow.

DREAM

Years ago I would often have a dream about something or someone, which would actually occur the next day, or at most within two days. This phased out by the time I was about fifty. My youngest daughter Wendy seems to have inherited this strange ability (if you can call it that! I don't know how else to describe it!), with prophetic dreams occasionally assailing her otherwise normal life.

Sometime in the early hours of Friday, 22 November 1963, I had a dream which was lucid enough to recall it in detail when I awoke in the morning. It began with me mingling with a happy group of people on a balcony. I joined them drinking cocktails whilst they were waiting for something to happen. An event which was for some sort of convoy to pass by. We were all looking expectantly over the balcony. I knew without doubt that we were in Texas, USA, and I remember wondering what on earth I was doing there.

The next part of the dream was an aftermath. I was observing the reactions of people who were walking in the street. I was actually in the street with them. They moved slowly, some in the middle of the road, all looking stunned.

Their faces had a dazed expression as they moved aimlessly around, shocked at what they had experienced. I don't know the reason for this. I was simply a bystander. I didn't get to know in the dream what had caused this profound effect.

Later that morning, after depositing my son at school, I called in to see my mother-in-law who lived very close to the school. For some reason, I mentioned my dream, possibly because the memory was still vivid. The day continued as normal, and in the evening, after settling the children down, I looked forward to watching *Route 66*, a popular programme on television. It was interrupted with an urgent and very shocking announcement that the president of the USA, John Kennedy, had just been assassinated. He had been shot in the head from a large building called the library, which I had seen clearly in my dream. I don't know why I only saw the build-up to the event and then the aftermath. I have to add that although I was saddened for the Kennedy family, the tragedy did not involve me deeply. I was truly just a spectator in my dream. It was a dream about people's reaction, rather than the actual event.

THE DRESS

Something that happened well over fifty years ago. It was typical of my many experiences, where I seemed to know only part of a situation, not the whole picture.

It was a Saturday. We still lived in Woking, Surrey and were between postings abroad. I can't remember who was babysitting for the children that weekend, but I clearly recall that our quest was to find a much longed-for bureau, and so my husband and I set off to busy Guildford, where we finally found our perfect bureau in a furniture shop at the top of the high street. We soon found what we were looking for there and were discussing the final approval of the desk when, out of the blue, I got a sudden clear picture of my elder daughter Shanny with blood spatters on the front of her dress. Alarmed, I told my husband, whereupon we left the shop in a hurry and hastened back to the parked car and then home. No mobile in those days! On our return home, we went into the kitchen just as Shanny, who was in the garden, passed by the window. Sure enough, the front of her dress was spattered with blood. She was unaware that there was even any blood at all. Well, the cause was soon revealed. Earlier, her rabbit had escaped once again. Shanny had recovered it and held it close to her chest. The rabbit had objected and struggled frantically, scratching at the dress and possibly getting its paws caught in the buttonholes of the dress. So, the blood belonged to the rabbit, and it appeared to be no worse for its ordeal. Shanny was completely unhurt by the rabbit's frantic efforts, so all was well!

We went back to the furniture shop to pay for and collect the bureau. My point is: why did I only see part of the picture? Why did I see blood on the dress so clearly, and yet Shanny was completely unharmed?

SIKH SHRINE

Once again, my husband was off to one of his many geophysical explorations. This time, it was West Pakistan. He stayed in the district of Chakwal. We had lived there about five and a half years before. Most of his work interest was in the nearby salt range. I liked that part of the world and wished I could have joined Richard on what would have been a nostalgic return to the past. His work would keep him there for about eight weeks. It seemed an interminable time for us to be separated. About halfway through his assignment, I decided one lonely night, just before going to bed, that I would visit Richard whilst I was still sleeping. A silly thought, I know, but it softened the absence. I've no idea what time it was when I found myself high in the air, looking down on unfamiliar territory. It looked like a large palace of some kind. It was surrounded by a great deal of water. It was an amazing sight, but I suddenly felt insecure hovering in space. I knew wherever it was, Richard was not there, so where was I? My quest was for Richard not the location! I wanted to return to the security of my bedroom, which I did immediately. Now comes the strange part! Meanwhile, my husband had found himself with a free day and decided on a sudden whim to visit a famous Sikh temple. It was, he said in his letter, *a top tourist attraction.* Incidentally, I had never heard of this shrine. Sikh pilgrims visited from all over India and Pakistan. It is situated about three miles from the Indo-Pakistan border.

The next day, I wrote a letter to my husband describing my dream journey to that shrine. Our letters crossed. It took about nine days for our letters to arrive. Richard gave me details about the shrine without even knowing that my night adventure had led me there. It was situated about one hundred and seventy miles from the Chakwal area, in a place called Shakargarh. Its name is Gurdwara Kartarpur. Pakistan is about five hours ahead of England, and I don't know the exact time I was transported in my dream, so I can't embroider on this 'happening'. I know that it wasn't very dark. I can't remember if there were people around. The surrounding water was the clincher. It convinced Richard that we had possibly, at the same time, shared our visit to the shrine. Certainly within a few hours.

Guru Nanak, founder of Sikhism. He was a very good man! The Guru's teaching has been peace and harmony. He believed in equality between castes, religions and gender and coined the Sikh symbol *Ik Onkar* (there is only one God!). A pity there are not more people like him in this world.

GUARDIAN ANGELS

We are all supposed to have a guardian angel, keeping us safe for twenty-four hours a day. That's a huge responsibility for an angel! I can't imagine how they were designated from our birth to protect us. I now believe that guardian angels are in fact the holy spirit. All too ineffable for us to comprehend, therefore I'll leave it at that!

A long time ago – sixty-three years in fact, when I lived in Baghdad, Iraq – something happened to me that I can only attribute to my guardian angel, 'holy spirit'.

I was taking a walk around the block, which included passing the American embassy. I must have been about five or six months pregnant at the time. We still had a curfew but were only restricted to just before dusk until early the following morning. On this occasion, I was just walking past the impressive gates to the embassy, which was now empty of all the American citizens. They had returned for safety to the USA. Suddenly, two armed soldiers approached. They grabbed me by the arms, one either side, and forced me into the embassy grounds. Probably taking me to their commander in charge. I thought naively, trying not to panic. They were marching me towards what looked like an abandoned building. Fear rose inside me as I realised their motives were not in the line of duty. Just as my fear was beginning to get a stranglehold, a man wearing an officer's uniform appeared, as if from nowhere, and was hurrying towards us. The two soldiers released their grip on my arms and actually moved away from me. The officer was shouting and seemed very angry with the two men. His speech was harsh, with a guttural sound, which often sounds angry to my ears, even when it's not, but on this occasion, it was rage! He dismissed them and they shuffled off rather than marched. I think being shamed had altered their gait! The officer then turned to me and gazed at me sternly but not unkindly. He pointed towards the large gate. "Go home immediately and don't come back again."

I didn't need to be told twice. I breathed a deep, audible sigh of relief and, forgetting to thank him, walked as fast as I could to the safety of my bungalow. No sign of the American marines across the road. Perhaps they had been called back to the states or were required for duty elsewhere.

Now, was that officer my guardian angel or did my guardian angel prompt the officer in some way. Or, as I believe, did the holy spirit protect me? Does he really send his angels to guard us? Why, then, isn't everyone protected from evil?

My granddaughter Sophie quite recently gave me a small guardian angel, which displays variegated colours like opals. I really like it but am reluctant to display it, in fear of being branded one of the bells and smell contingents which incidentally, referring to smell! Incense is used far more often now in the Anglican church! Not sure where the bells come in!

The Catholic church has tried hard to appease the Protestant church's criticisms in the past. They accuse the Catholics of worshipping Our Lady, the mother of God. What ignoramuses not to find out the facts! Catholics respect, honour and love Mary, *not* worship. Only God is allowed to be worshipped. Magistrates and Mayers are addressed as your worshipful. It's simply a matter of semantics!

The electrician who warned me of impending danger in my kitchen seventeen years ago, was he an angel? I strongly believe now that he was! I didn't turn my head to look at him. I just listened and was heedful to his succinct warning.

I made little effort to learn the exotic names of shrubs and flowers. I recognise them but do not respond to their long Latin names given by some bright herbert. I can't remember who the poet was that wrote an appealing poem about a tiny seashell. He said:

> *...a learned man / could give it a clumsy name. / Let him name it who can, / the beauty would be the same...*

I don't feel that I'm enthusiastic anymore about making people laugh. I'm not sure if it's getting old and lacking energy, or just not caring so much if people are sad or happy. I prefer to think it's the former!

I've enjoyed writing the fragmented autobiography. I am not well known or famous in any way. My life has not been earth moving, but I have had a large share of love, for which I am truly thankful. I don't know why I was widowed almost forty years ago. I don't know why my husband was taken at only fifty-three. There are many souls who have endured a similar fate. I will never understand why so many people have to suffer sadness in this world, but I do know that we all will be part of the perfect pattern. I have glimpsed it!

SUMMING UP

Well, I may not make people laugh anymore, but I hope that some parts of my story will make you smile. Remember to pray, hope and not worry. If I could ask for anything in this world, it would be to give my children and grandchildren the gift of faith. There is no greater legacy.

It is no great thing to live long nor even to live forever, but it is a great thing to live well.

St Augustine of Hippo 354–430